In a Time of No Song

**JEFF
BIEN**

In

a

Time

of

No

Song

INTRODUCTION BY

A.F. MORITZ

EXILE
editions

Library and Archives Canada Cataloguing in Publication

Bien, Jeff, 1957-, author
In a time of no song / Jeff Bien ; introduction by A.F. Moritz.

Poems.
Issued in print and electronic formats.
ISBN 978-1-55096-476-9 (pbk.).--ISBN 978-1-55096-479-0 (pdf).--
ISBN 978-1-55096-477-6 (epub).--ISBN 978-1-55096-478-3 (mobi)

I. Title.

PS8553.I353I5 2015   C811'.54   C2015-900875-1
                                          C2015-900876-X

Design and Composition by Mishi Uroboros
Cover Photograph *Désir - Montréal, 1982/2010* by Serge Clément
Typeset in Cambria, Minion, Harrington and Zapfino fonts at Moons of Jupiter Studios

Published by Exile Editions Ltd ~ www.ExileEditions.com
144483 Southgate Road 14-GD, Holstein, Ontario, N0G 2A0
Printed and Bound in Canada in 2015, by Marquis Books

We gratefully acknowledge, for their support toward our publishing activities,
the Canada Council for the Arts, the Government of Canada through
the Canada Book Fund (CBF), the Ontario Arts Council,
and the Ontario Media Development Corporation.

Canadian Sales: The Canadian Manda Group, 664 Annette Street,
Toronto ON M6S 2C8 www.mandagroup.com 416 516 0911

North American and International Distribution, and U.S. Sales:
Independent Publishers Group, 814 North Franklin Street,
Chicago IL 60610 www.ipgbook.com toll free: 1 800 888 4741

For Rafi
and that one word that abides in every other.

The Silence of a Word

The History of the Unknown World

Falling From the Blue Tree

Stars

II

From the Book of Angels

The Metafictions of Om

From the Book of Imaginary Letters

As the Black Rose Sings

A Few Words for
In a Time of No Song

To those who know Jeff Bien's poetry, it's a secret treasure they wish weren't so secret. *In a Time of No Song* is a substantial introduction to this *sui generis* poet, who can be well characterized by applying to him his own words from "Catching silver":

> *You are already that magician in the desert,*
> *red berries falling from your hand*

The book is divided into ten parts, each a coherent, impassioned small book in itself, and these ten parts are gathered in two large sections of six and four. The density – the relentless beauty and provocation – of Bien's verse makes the separations valuable: the almost overwhelming flow of the poetry can be grasped at first in terms of each of these parts, works in themselves and yet inseparable from the whole.

What is this poetry like? There are not many precedents for it or bodies of work very similar to it in English. Maybe it can best be approached through a sample. For instance:

> *Dipping their nets, they hear only the sea speckled in pride*
> *mending the barrios of the grand and open sky*
> *what betrays itself, at last, in the bruised and busking earth*
> *that commonwealth which lovers lie upon, rumpled in time about.*
> ...
> *Then give me words for what we cannot praise,*
> *and let secrets bleed our bleeding hearts away,*
> *and there against the sound of clemency*
> *plant fear into the grid of a songbird's mouth.*

These are lines from "The untitled way – for Dylan Thomas." We might say that Bien's poetry is a little like Dylan Thomas's: the combination of imagistic and metaphoric richness with a stylistic drive that turns grammatical and rhetorical complexity into a fiery lava flow and simultaneously the upward spring of a shady, gently resounding tree.

Bien's word hoard is all his own, though, the way he animates it, constantly connecting the outer with the inner, the familiar with the distant, the limited with the vast, the realm of thought with the realm of life, non-sentient things with sentient ones. The sea has pride (which is the foam of its combers and breakers), the sky has barrios, the earth though bruised still busks (and we hear Hopkins: all is "bleared, smeared with toil" by us and yet "nature is never spent; / There lives the dearest freshness deep down things"), the earth is a commonwealth (Bien's phrase gives a Wordsworthian double meaning to the word – it becomes both a government and a source of "joy in widest commonalty spread"), the commonwealth is a rumpled bed of lovers, clemency makes its own sound, secrets do their own planting and what they plant is fear.

There is scarcely a stanza in Bien's work that does not contain some instance of these extendings and plunges into each other performed by things and whole modes of existence. More notable still is the mysterious ease with which the poems admit the contradictions present in perceptions, emotions and desires. The two stanzas quoted are a fusion of pleasure and foreboding that expresses the little recognized simultaneity of these things in our hearts. There's something of this fusion in the very fact that the second of the stanzas is a prayer which is calmly interpersonal in tone, confident in an aiding presence, while what it asks is to acknowledge and speak things that we cannot possibly think are good. This is said in the first line and repeated with enhancing difference in the last, where the very voice of the songbird, symbol and reality of our enchantment with the best of nature, is asked to express fear, and is called a "grid," referencing the standardization wrought by the technological world.

This evil and others linked to it form one element of Bien's vision, though far from the basic one, which is beauty and the thirst for beauty. In his 1996 collection *America & other poems*, a poem named "As the Walls Came Down" (evoking the Berlin Wall as well as the whole symbolism of "wall") has these couplets:

...there were ghosts, and a thousand armies quarrelling
over what went wrong in the hearts of men.

...

undergraduates with baccalaureate degrees
swooning to their own benign recitations of grief

as nations burst into flames
and the song went on being written.

It's hard to conceive of a more open-eyed and grieving definition of humanity's plight in "a time of no song," when relative peace and security has been established, but the new reality is made up of ghosts of ideas and ideals, the empty but bitter contention of conflicting shallow claims and ideologies, the current tendency of education to trivia, the production of personalities unable to distinguish even in their own motives between sincerity and exigent, self-deluding hypocrisy. Yet at the end of the quotation, there appears the hope almost left unnoticed in the bottom of the Pandora's box we've opened. Bien gives us back the persistence of the song, even in the face of all the false and empty songs that are taken for the true one.

In 1996, simultaneously with *America*, Bien published a second collection, *Prosody at the Cafe du Coin*, which counterbalances the long, prophetic political poems of *America* with a mysterious lyricism. Yet the links between the two books are clear. Certain poems in *Cafe* connect to *America* in displaying the wreck of materialism, and especially in delineating the plight of poetry, and all the liveliness it stands for, within that enervating ruin. It is a place where "only a tongue might rise / from the pale tragedy" ("In a City of Avalanches") and yet the human tongue has let itself be seduced and traduced by society's lack of energy: "Once it spoke of freedom and immortality / Now it jealously guards its itinerary" (title poem). But in *Cafe* more than in *America* the purpose is not to unveil the spiritlessness of contemporary culture but to move us to a grander and more open sky:

And angels and still more angels
gather in these tiny hours

of hierarchy and truth
and angels
who know poetry is pure sentience
and laughter godliness.

There again is Hopkins's freshness that lives within things, though they may only be a minuscule item or moment, a narrow crack in the all-smothering membrane that is our civilization: "these tiny hours / of hierarchy and truth." Bien's opening of the cell door here shines out even on the level of the single word. With an explosion of light, "hierarchy" leaps from its role as a description of bureaucracy, usually implying criticism, to the dignity of its underlying meaning, rule by a high priest, and now, in this case, one who is a valid high priest: truth. The move from one meaning to the other is the axis of Bien's vision.

In a Time of No Song will impress readers with its poetry of pure sentience and godlike laughter, but its richness may seem almost overwhelming. Can we make a map of this flowering forest of a book? The title of Part 1, "In a Time of No Song," seems meant to remind us of the famous statement by the German Romantic poet Friedrich Hölderlin, in his "Bread and Wine," asking "what are poets for in destitute times," to cite the most common English version, the one used in the translation of Martin Heidegger's essay "What Are Poets For?" Christopher Middleton marvelously translates, "what's to be done or be said / I do not know, or the object of poets in desolate times." Bien portrays the situation in his book's first poem, its title poem:

I too love the Odes, the smell of nutmeg in a lover's eye
the orphaned fragrance that chases the silent letters about the universe
and leaves behind no miracle story, or muted sound, only the weeping mortar
of the pyramid of knowledge, that is moonlight's narrow bridge.

The Odes seem to have become an elusive essence, chasing silence and incapable now of giving us a story and a miracle, not even the remote trace of one; there is nothing but the sorrow created by the opaque material of a giant entombing monument to a knowledge that does not give life. And yet, seemingly paradoxically, this knowledge itself contains some good, retains for us an immured trace of the imagination.

There is still a champion of life in this desolate time: "In the scrapyard of prayer, a holy rascal, a starling, … the royal self that remembers no rose, or lover, or speaking at all, / and I its nagging singer." This is our faithfulness to the Odes. It might seem at first that the common, scorned city bird *is* the poet, but then the poet emerges *in propria persona*, and it is clear that the bird, while his image, is also an Other who confronts and joins him, a member of community with him, his image yet his brother, who gives him a friend and a model, who saves him from isolation and narcissism. To assert, seek, achieve a community of those who yearn for life is grasped as central throughout the poem ("I too love the way the snow…"; "I will play you my instrument…"; "I will give you…"; "I too love the taste…") as it reaches its concluding hope:

> *an orchard of lovely berries singing on a dying tree*
> *and so all the while, so too, I sing, that which sings me, in a time of no song.*

I don't want to go too far into interpretation. I'll just say that the tension established here, between the deathly limiting force of what (we think) we know and the threatened but poetically defended thrust towards a more ample life and worldview, undergirds *In a Time of No Song*.

In the first major section (six suites) the poems suffer and fight out this opposition to its resolution in a hope that is perhaps no more certain at the end than at first, except in that the poet has been true to it through a long struggle. At the end of the final suite, a brief poem concludes with a behest that condenses what we have been through in this poetry. The ravaged firmament, it says, is also, mysteriously, "The royal light that turns a page," and by that light we should "see in the…most beautiful of all, the beholder itself." I especially like "itself." The word "beholder" usually conveys to us that *we* are the beholder vis-à-vis "objective reality," but with a shock we realize that there is another beholder here.

The second major section (four suites) plunges in again, as if recognizing that the achievement of the first section is still too removed, and must be put into action in life among "the things that cannot be changed or left unchanged"

("Caravanserai"). There, even desolation itself is a piece of luck, to live it on this earth – "My cup runneth over with emptiness" ("Song") – and we glimpse the fullness possible, even inherent, in emptiness, a theme that the presence of tribute poems to Hafiz and Rumi signals. The mysticism of the source is here, but most of all, I think, we will remember the great enactments and themes of this book through its omnipresent, brilliant tributes to life: "the clouds draping a bareheaded sun...the Andalusian blue that cannot be untold ("Song")." We'll keep it by us for its indelible celebrations in the midst of difficulties, personal and social, that are fully, direfully admitted:

> *While deconstructed go all the tides, a wordsmith without a word,*
> *even now in disbelief, a teacher's moon,*
> *caught in the tattle of a river*
> *that thoughtless perfects the wretched light.*
>   —"Churchless coming"

A.F. MORITZ

I

In
a
Time
of
No
Song

In a time of no song

I too love the Odes, the smell of nutmeg in a lover's eye
the orphaned fragrance that chases the silent letters about the universe
and leaves behind no miracle story, or muted sound, only the weeping mortar
of the pyramid of knowledge, that is moonlight's narrow bridge.

And in the scrap yard of prayer, a holy rascal, a starling,
cobalt in a shining purple gown, a shawl for the one who wears its nakedness
the royal self that remembers no rose, or lover, or speaking at all,
and I its nagging singer, a widow's hump on my back.

These are the poems that have no poet, the thimble of moon in a wineskin
the famished sun whirling the dervishes
the cherry glass that shatters rainbows into a thousand chattering birds,
singing the way of love, the guru of every language but one.

I cherish the hayfields, where the unscholarly sleep beneath the pinwheel of stars
a white fleece of ember dreaming a bur of quiet cobbling its path,
the weighing of flesh in the market stalls, and the flaying of a martyr's tongue
the tempest that cries out in stone, the rain that is the heart beating.

I too love the way the snow sleeves its way into a rose-shaped breath
children, like lambs, bleating a wild view of everything at once,
hushed by the pastoral sonnets, a blanket of leaves, a bedding of soft hands,
and a word that has never been spoken.

I followed the past, the lidless eye, the limbs of Adam's soul
the pangs of mystery in the womb house of three kisses,
a sail of tall sadness, the throat song of ecstasy, listening quietly
by the green throne of those who have never been loved.

I will play you my instrument, and then immolate all that I am
I will give you this lonely idol, that I have smashed, death mask of bone on bone
I too love the taste of toasted chestnuts and the dark task of a winter's night
the sweetest of the bitter herbs, and the wild honey that has no taste at last.

A dove lands on my shoulder, the unbearable weight of magic
what shelters each moment in every other, dies and lives, homelessly on,
an orchard of lovely berries singing on a dying tree
and so all the while, so too, I sing, that which sings me, in a time of no song.

A bribe for the ferryman

The river in the morning with its mist
high above the sky, tap tuning the curly bird's eye maple

with its falconer's hand
lifting the windmills into the white face of the dove.

On the easel of angels, face painting colours
diving into that stilled mirror of the gods

the red fleet of morning ship song,
feathered glass tail of the sun,

where you are there, in the nothing that listens,
whisper singing where no one hears.

I bribed the ferryman with love
and the tempters with bread.

In the temple of Athena I froze time
into cherry blossoms that fell like a lover's eyelids.

I rode the black Pegasus into the tent of blue song
that is lovingly born

bowing to the instrument,
the sink wood of the cello's sparrow neck

the begging bowl of the drum,
the seafarer's rhyme in the water lines and tiger strings,

rounding the belly of the laughing Buddha
the true Islamic angels of the loneliest sunset.

The crocuses crow beneath snow,
the beginning of words melting in our eyes

the stars collapsing each time we say I do
the miracle talk of night spoons, and giant scorpion moons

the pirouetting kiss of the heavens, that bribed the ferryman
kissing each sadness away, and the word made flesh

that watches over love.

Sometimes

Sometimes we can't see the orphaned starling
its breast feathers, the plumage of a desert sun.

And sometimes we sing above that stray wind
that is the miraculous quiet moon of our breath.

Slowly we run into the burning bush,
to recite the names of emptiness, and be that sailing fire.

And sometimes when the saints come, we are in the brothel, falling
into the blackest rose, and living like the holy one in its petals,

Our hearts shackled to that old rag of love
that is the exilic psalm, in that curious place that cannot be hidden.

Sometimes with one coin in our pocket rainbows arise,
the blunt saber of a tall and golden shadow,

On windowsills and on the table where clockmakers tinker
the early hour of birds, and an arabesque of chattering stars.

Sometimes a singing hill rises by the old river mill
buying your love, and you are a warrior again.

You ask and ask, in that everlasting palace of white
in your midnight garden singing,

The way a prisoner not yet free sings
in her unanswerable darkness,

And a bird with paper wings has crept through the bars,
quietly pleading, carrying a note that has no name.

An eyelash for the moon

How does the chrysalis grow, the sunlight
Scrambled in the calves' eyes, in the worried leaves,
In the amnesty of insects' wings.

And earth-like things arise, open-eyed in death's death
Sailing in beloved poems, that will never speak a word
Everything mushroomed into the net of ash, and the blue sleeve of yes.

Yet return and return, half within, tinkered inside
Two square centimetres of cobalt in the coat of her eyes
Cut from the shoulder of a rainbow.

I will leave you three words, for a symphony of spring
I will go into your heart and never return
It is snowing on the honey plants, I will pitch my tent there forever.

A fire wasp has come into the casino night
Eulogizing the breeze that flows from the dead sea, where not far away winter prays
And that is you kneeling, kissing a grain of sand, an inch above the tide.

In every heart-whisperer, the lazy eye of faith leaps, maddeningly tilts
Tillandsias dance in the air, flowers that breathe without earth
As you must learn breath, in the vineyard that has no ancient book.

In the African violets, grey is white without angels, splintering
In the slowness that wanders, as death begins to tease,
Inescapable, like a lover's brutal delight.

A golden sloth arrives in the pixie blue plants
Put your hands in that little happiness
Find the singer, that has no song, be lifted into its tireless praise.

This twilight I have known

The blue-throated hummingbird, a suddenness in the fleece of air
Needle pointing a quiet fury of wings
Tiny bells of wilderness shining the stars
Coat-hanging a rainbow of sky

Everywhere love streaming holographs of slender seashells and topaz,
A ratchet of threads, spangled cockles, orange-peeled sun angels, angling a trail of light

The muff of winter tales, wood nymphs and the Long-Eared Owl
Flutter bugs and pea moths, reeling, always with a hundred widow singers

And the diamond-backed twigs that fall in the thimble of snapdragons
Running into the blackened half-moon

This twilight I have known, the tuft of white dwarfs skidding, crayoning the perch of day
The flappers' high step, a dragonfly stiller than a river stone

Strumming deeply the tiniest fragrance
Of sage and blood weather, humble bees pluming the carnival glass tides

Cerise scintillated auburn forewarned into magic,
Finger-pointing the three slow wishes, in the tallest oaken pew

A scribe for the tail feathers of ferns and seed grass
A crooked beastly thing, twines itself in the twain of night

The bend of it, half sliced with the stray church mouse preaching
As the mystical hour arrives

Dog pale-faced and flame footed
They dance like song.

Tillandsias

Like lovers they grow in air, fragrant hours of colours
Sunning an unexpected word,
Turning in the buckshot of a slow dying moon
Handwringing the voice of the coriander.

Falling upwards into the pinnacle where the cradle of hush begins
Leave the word to write the word, they plead, and the painter unpainted
Their wand brings the magician to her knees, animal like
Namelessly whispering the colloquialism of the sacred, looking up.

The blue sky is cancelled by the glare of a red hill
Cold winds cuddle, a net of thunderbolts in their side
Wingless in the hourglass of the river, how soon they will be at work,
Leaping backwards leaving the wedding behind.

This is how it all began, the small talk of the leprechauns
Beginningless death, my own death, the collapsed language of civilization
That sits in rainbow pose by white sands, while in the slums
And refugee camps, the marriage ceremony of the work of midnight stars.

If only the laughter that bends with the snow, the oblivion of the quiet fleeing
The flags burning, the voiceless flask of thanksgiving
A simple mantra from above, recited in an old monk's shack
Nowhere seemingly heard, a thimble for the finger pointing to the moon.

The miller's wheat, more expensive than gold, in a time of famine
The empty silos, a spindle of soul tilting, shining red steeples calling out to a god
The book of manna, miracle of quail and snow in a desert, and unleavened bread
Eve flew into air, captured by three angels, drunk on the allegorical mysteries.

He has left with the story, the storyteller
No high and narrow silence, no mind in mind,
Everything already returned to a paradise of tailing suns,
A song moving on a beam of sunlight.

So I awake from the nightmare of day and night, and day
Whisper invictus to whatever is not listening and know I must ever look back
Lips everywhere, everywhere children dying, and those unscholarly airborne flowers
Crawling upwards longitudinally, like a single blade of grass.

The homeless of Canaan

I marvel at the thunder,
the plumped up feathers of the pheasant's soft voice

the black tar that shines the milk glass moon
and the mountain stream that sires the gold.

The grey slate of the wave, curling in its ear
all that will not listen,

the hand that polishes the heart shaped leaf
and lifts the view, the bugler's eye closed.

I marched into that weather, the homeless of Canaan,
small drummer boy that I was,

in perfect rinds of psalm and Godspeed
reeling in the lock houses, the thin republic of dream.

Running into the away, breathlessly in the oceans bright
famous with the cockleshells and puffer fish

and rock pebblers that I passed on my twilight ride
the July flowers in June, the suffocating night breeze combing the shore.

Jerusalem was young then, and I taller than my shadow
wrestling the ghosting eves down.

I was like David with Bathsheba
the round dance of clay in the potter's hand.

On a mule, headless in the oak tree's bough,
where warless meets war, and wanderers rest,

in the torture rooms with no angel's peeping eye
reciting only this, *have you loved enough.*

There I lay, with the view of the sea
the sound of the hammer dulcimer, chanting on the tide.

How many times since, have I said song
how many times, lovers, beggars, angels and death.

Sewing the white thread into black
that buttons the eyes of the rag doll,

that smallish library, one torn page turning another
undivided dove-like perfections born.

And there with the shepherds watching
over the sweetest ground, the sitting bones of sunlight

the braille of a dusking silence,
naked and prayer the same.

Sweet gentle rain

Sweet gentle rain, hand fallen
the fields upturned in their poorest clothes
the black-faced songbird on the rail fences,
an opera of sulking gods, fire ladder red.

In the theatre of the moon garden, the gills of the parrot fish,
voiceless cellos and windswept small-eyed paths,
a gallop of tattling unfamiliar sounds, fruit moths rope laddered to an anthem of mangy light
a foolish rainbow of never ending silence.

And here where all things run from that one-sided breath
that curls into a spine of runaway stars, a gaffe of two sleepless eyes
the curfew of a word that begs the hollowed quiet,
the voiceless pews in that field of spangled night.

The organ grinders sway, lost in the half-starved village
ten thousand hyacinths by the mosque's gilded door,
a colour wheel of kite strings busking in the autumn leaves
tinselled by the neon tinctures and the tallness growing homelessly there.

Oh, improvised fire of every lover's hand
I have the scripture of the river, tattered as a broken heart
and the untravelled, unbraided wodge of day flowers
spears of peasant green and foolhardy nuptial yellow, cloudlessly blue as the hillside of sea.

In the Bantustan orchards where nations are born
a thousand candles burning on the birthday of Rome
an infant star on molten stilts in the early morning hour
one tiny planet, one wishful wish-kissing stone.

The dark night face painting a laughing crow
tinkering with sugar plums, mugged in the litmus of air
and the round dance of words that damn one another,
the bumbleweeds glum-eyed song, a glooming scripture that would not hear our plea.

Small paper ships like sleepless sheep unfolding in a crease of twilight
scudding beneath a gallows moon, a wave of trees, fossils that mime cave walls,
hearing no singer of that fever of sound, that fragrance of rain
the cloud scent of hill stations and weeping barren lands.

In the book of mystery, parchment of white spirited moths
a sea of rumpled small hours, a warren of angels creeping
in the gold leaves of the sweet hereafter and freshly fallen snow,
rag merchants, punch-drunk, plié in a mud house of celestial light.

One thread unravelling, in each scrap of the universe,
secret guide of the singing, in the bluish mums, glory operas disappearing
in the witching nocturnal thunders, rallying cry of the yet unborn,
blood and treasure, in the sweet gentle rain.

Listen

Listen to the sermon of the bell
Listen to the auburn days of the white elm
Listen to the tiniest leaves, the braille of small roses, counted like mala beads
Twigging the soundless sound, imaginary hollows cribbed in secrets.

Listen to the country roads shadow-leaping the bleeding blue high throne
Listen to the mirth of wind, tickling the foliage
The brass wings of fire immolating the black-tailed moth
Listen to your enemy, listen as if you were a child, watching a starling eye the robin's nest.

Listen with cats' ears to the soft paw of the night sky, the waif of moon, braiding a sailor's knot
Listen to the outrageous colours uprooting the greens and yellows
Listen to the way the crabapples fall softly, red as rain drops
Silver backs running upstream from the sea.

Listen to the cradle of water hymn, in the fire trail of the bulrushes
Listen to the dwarfish ponies, slowly moving drifts of snow,
The woollen eyes of old owls that see a mouse's breath, listen this way
Like a Bedouin who can track a grain of sand, in the roundabout moment before dawn.

Listen to the Navaho listening to the pathless red star,
A wishing stone in the love blur of wind,
Stitching the smallness that rescues a magnificent joy
Put an arrow to your heart and listen well.

Listen to the lover's hand, listen by the empty well, as if the Word were listening
Listen to the long crease line of laughter in her eyes.
Let love be your listening
Listen to her moan, she is a beautiful prayer.

Listen to the death of the second hand, the minute hand, the hour hand
The murky guest in its stowaway of meaning
Listen to the lanterns grow dark in the sun, wicks of geese returning home
Listen to the slowness of late afternoon clouds, dayflowers perfectly tuned.

Listen to the children, the shoreless cries from the shanty town,
Listen as if the clouds that touch the fields were the ogling of a perfect bending
And rising blade of grass, a stipend of grey starlight, growing young and old
Listen deeply to your own listening, listen, without listening, and be heard.

Squaw
Duck
for
the
Bard

Hunchback

I am crippled now, a hump made of rags
I know it is true, when the shipping fields
run over the crackling sounds,
and the hunched over buttercups mutter my name.

And when we speak for the first time
impossible shadows burning themselves down
in the bonfire of the meadow.
That longish book, on eggshells and numberless winters written.

I want not to touch you, with all the eloquence of
the lowing wind, roughing itself to the sea.
Shaped by orphaned constellations, in the hilling grass
moving them, the sun yoked to its plough.

I know too, how the broken hearts mend, and a first kiss
a prisoner's map, the curled lines
where other hands have lain
the long dystopian night where nothing emptied sleeps.

But lofts of crows, watched from afar,
the fuselage of light, the purple in the thimble weeds
and ever barren tree,
the girding stake from which love looks down.

Overseer of the dewless night
the spinning bees and star fruit
the crucified paper cities, the dowelling of the universe
crying still, to the one thing above.

If I have tasted this voice, only this voice
in the awful half-stilled nights,
crooked in the memory, in the splitting of a hair
the parable of a pneumonic sea.

And played again, on her tinfoil lips, the music box
of angels and beggars and rags,
after all asking for more than one word,
and in empty wombs, drunken lovers born.

Squaw duck for the bard

for Purdy

You were at the top of the world
where the high tides begin

foot-tangled in a thimble of moon,
the hatched song of the tiniest word

and that old squaw duck with her glockenspiel silences
pearling the long-tailed light.

Praising on your loom
the jeweled lichen and arctic flowers,

reeling the deathless bird song
hawking the wildest season.

Old bird, old squaw, you sang
with a billy can of stars, dwarf willows

and spanless time. The stubby-eyed prairie tundra
lifted into the golden wheat in Christ's eye

the dog song of the Sabbath angel craning
from your hands.

Hungover in the whisky glass morning
the cabin fever of blue yoked to blue

that grew into orange sunsets
and flockless geese lost in the god-minded stone.

There in the jackstraw of colours
the sun's ropes like red garters

the snow daisies and wedding frost
arrowed in the heel of night.

The toy sea, the church song of bees
the silk throwers with their broken winged gods.

Young night, first night, you chanted,
the snake rumour in you rhyming the days old

haggling with the fence straddling selves,
the high-winged logos and curling gondolas of snow,

the dog-eared blur of Faustian night
the onionskin largo that sheds its mighty sound.

You might find Jerusalem in the open air,
bone throwing miracles (winter turning the brown rabbit white).

The mewing letter of wordlessness
the horse-traders who lift their cups to that running emptiness,

wild combs of starlight, the colour of peafowl,
in that jamboree of snow crystals and perfect light.

The blessed winter scholars
who made texts of its eyes,

and a singing bird
the ghost writer of their song.

All night long I waited

All night long I waited for the fictional bird
Noah's dove, or the raven that fed Elijah.

I looked for that line that circles the hawkish one,
quieting the tall tales the saddhus speak of.

When they passed the hat to the whaling silences
the house was in bloom, thin necked in feathers.

A hundred poems lay about me
like still grass, half-asleep, sailors of love.

In a softly begging wind
the hammer watch that tinkers with the eggshell blue,

the steel bones of the unicorn
and the white tail feathers of a wainscoted sky.

The fanning peacocks, bell ropes and sunless coral graves
and a swing far away ever coming,

yoking the soul to a drop of rain,
flooding the mannequin earth.

At night I long to hear the footprints in snow
the long beak of winter, that freezes the spigots of maple.

You are with me in the climbing morning dew,
dousing the twigging colours,

the staff I walk with to the pasture
in the twisting allegory of green

pointing to the high wire of lonely command
of halted towering river song.

The wind kissing the ferns, softly leaning,
the rock moss moonlighting there

the unspeakable unfolding, hunched over a pirated faith,
burning the effigies of itself.

Again untitled

When I first wrote the song
straw angels on my shoulder.

The blush of a rolling fragrance ramming the summer air
a loop of starlight inside me ran amuck.

Small birds gossiping amongst the snapping twigs
in the tailspin of blood and treasure.

And I, writing love letters to that same hymn
storytelling its sadness, the wand of it everywhere.

Patiently green in the yard sales of ripened sounds
the yellowed hills of a quiet knowledge.

It is a beginning, I would say to myself
and could hear the seas in each other being born.

Night calls, and on one wild knee, I kneel
kissing the books like a sweetheart's hand.

Late in the mystic hour, heir of that willing song
on the high country roads, each shadow red.

I place that word on a shingle above the trove of my shop door
tall oaks in a walrus's singing eye.

In the whole of the forest, slownesses praying
tags of quiet fury and quarried crags of soiled blue.

I was blessed the day I died, watching the lay of the land
the small songbird in my hand.

Asking for nothing at all,
so quiet, not even I could tell what it was singing.

How I tamed the universe with song

No workhorses on the first day of light
winter in my hair, her voice thin like rain.

I drew golden spirals, the noose of the tree, sacred geometry,
figures in the groan and whisper of a prophet's wife.

While I could have saved one thing from one other
I sang to that voice, the chattering class calls thugs.

Song, of mighty song, I chanted in Babylon's prison
as I surrounded Gomorrah.

The breath under my breath, when the grouse flew,
the moon around my neck, the glass slipper almost green.

Found in the moment after the moment of red
naked as any day.

The pillared hemispheres, springing in the air
spinning into sunset, summer tides falling.

Squid black, the ghetto minders of every birth
cut from the same fine cloth scrap traders call rags.

And become, become, become, king of the world
splendorous as night, cinched in quiet groves.

The one who fired the coloured glass for the moon saviour
the never-ending Herodian exile.

Dressed in the uniform of no return
when there was only the exodus of a long universal prayer.

The sun like squat brown grass
like the square of light my cat sits in, when the morning Buddha arrives.

Armageddon

So you stood on the small back of a bird
one hand on the reign, chasing fire to the end of the world.

Husking death with thumb cymbals and gaunt weed,
a sea of green chestnuts and the fabled cry that has ever borne deafness,

pirates who, folding clouds into rogue waves,
blackened the hands of the bronze maker.

And you stood on that narrow pole bridge where the Buddha stood,
the local storyteller widow-making the story.

And yes, to the promised land
you go with honey, and prayer, and a ribbon cutting song

though the prisoners sing all night long, in the open air
where you would rest if only you were poor enough again.

So it is the thinly peddled wonder that tugs on the sleeve,
when Christ that lonely Jew falls, like a bird in the well.

Your rags are like that, a nation, torn, stillborn, orphaned colours
bleeding into one, Odin hung from the world tree.

On the bank of a river where the cities grew into lovers' eyes
blazened in fire-irons of love, rough edging the word.

Penny bards rattling away, stealing the soundless,
plying the notes of the weathered music of climbing vines.

How many times, it repeats blue and sky, and darkness.
How the dancing girl and the young ones carve their names

The herdsman, in his turban of snakes,
chariot deities that ride the caliphate of that widowless night.

A soft wind against the cheek, a frond of light
pulling from our hand, the consort of Krishna

the fire rod and the fire, the sky with three full moons
the skull of lava, a paper cut in the white skin of the mountain

and the fear that grieves god, brought down
in the poorhouse that feeds that endless mystic chant.

With my naked eye

I sent a monk with bright white feathers
to carry the glass case of one of my songs.

For three thousand roses
I traded my pen, and was given a flute and wild horses to ride.

With my naked eye I saw things as they are
Rama with his myriad name, soldiers with gossamer wings

unwritten words gathered in warring colours
songs where no songs exist.

Foot pads gathered in the clouds, storytellers
with the small feet of the wind,

dressed in gifts and eloquent weather,
a hat of wishbones and seashells curled like night stars,

a thunderbolt hooked in my sleeve
asterisks of tree light, shaped by damselflies

who step-dance above, circling like red hawks
the river stone that sits like student monks.

A merchandise of sand made of fallen leaves
heaps of everlasting time,

where the unwed grass blooms into temple cities
and all about the world, its paper cut, and warm season.

Grist wheel of green, where steel and iron
were given name.

Surreal was I, that sought the city of "I"
by this bright gate, the overseer of one grain of sand.

The opera glass night,
the mystic poet that never sleeps

ghost whispering a night twisted so thin
cradling its long book of love before it.

And in the widowed streets of Rome
where I could still breathe and walk, and call my body my own.

Now everything is Buddha, the Pentecostal choirmaster,
the mouse, the chimes on the broken clock

the sarcophagi of sun that warms the painted turtle
and the orangutans, the triangles of chatter

that move like truth amongst swifter lies,
the acropolis of sky, one long sigh

raging against nothing at all.
And then resting the scythe of my arms in the moon,

laying my sickly head on a rock
singing before the "I" was born

creaking about the shepherdless universe,
all ado amongst nothing, moves on.

The
Silence
of
a
Word

The silence of a word

Here is my beggar's bowl and orphaned heart
filled with unopened letters and honey.

Here a fly's wing, like Amadeus who learned from a lark the song of wood
a blackened bird that remains in that dream.

At the tethered end of kite strings, the silence of a word,
Neruda counting the quiet till the twelfth of dawn.

The robins are back with their Hebrew scrolls
the flute of Krishna, its reddened fruit tied as a bow.

The last word I saw on a snow-eyed poplar's wing
catkin scribe to a beautiful illusion.

I have nothing to give back but this,
the ever ending understanding of self.

Birds nest there, where a day ago we disappeared
bees kissing bees, the tellers of history, curled like a cat.

In the well that appears, a laughing starlight,
the cloth of an inquisitor's gown giving flight.

The rustle of sky in the river we have always been,
parched lips counting beads.

The echo of ourselves unyoked, tossing stone,
the crest of water where it lands.

Poems

How little I understand of them
their tiny wild anguishes riddled into a flag like joy
grinding lenses of the feeble hours,
wandering into Galilee on Jerusalem's blind mule
and bending a grace note into the unannounced light.

How they go on cheerfully rattling their cages
telling the same forgetful story
the penny songs of Baruch Spinoza
and how Leibnitz gathered horse feathers at the Rhine.

And how they sing against a public meaning
a pantheon of rumour warbling into homelessness
cleaving the light
with tin bugles and frost-like hands.

How they are orphans of everything
the brightness of blue and red
uncoloured ribbons tied
into bitter and solemn deed,
their purse of envy stolen
as half-dressed they go out into night.

Their language is any language
bits of starlight and a rainmaker's secret heart
mantra stones and bone orchards huddled in rags,
flame alphabets and salt ruins
in a sewing box of sparrow's names.

How they sit on the page
like old superstitions,
with their unusual lockets and chalk-like mercies
and the nagging story of what Moses saw.
A secret architecture blooming on their lips.

In the graceyards with the kettles singing
and the long sabbatical of the unnamed,
by the rat tail of morning
a pantomime of long skirted parables and autumn colour.

How they are punished by love's magisterial names
their likenesses exalted by a prisoner's song,
lulled to sleep like roses
in the bent hours and conference of their veins.

A sublime anarchy high above them, untitled
in the poor villages where they have lost their way.

Oh, I have torn from their hands a prickly night
fell in love with their scholarly fool's gold
tricked into a night of believing
the fruit more than the seed.

Then forgive them their hope
and ballerina-like faith,
the ramparts of silence
where they build their altars
to Valhalla and Rome.

In the still hours their fleets battering a shore
a flagless march upon a towerless name,
a song from the cliff dragged under
a travelling light.

For the letters

If the yellow bird comes, and the wedding gift is returned
If under a small tree I am wearing my fedora

If I dig under the lilies
to bury my letters of silence

If all the world turns blue, like an iguana
on the night before the burning season.

If for seven years I am blessed with famine
and a stranger comes as a song on my lips

If I rejoice at the fearless symmetry
that awakens the never-sleeping sun,

and the shoeless storytellers
are given name.

And if in the chamber of unhewn stone
as the stars slip away and the coyote sings

I dream of a vineyard
where the exile gathers

and all that is green sleeps on
like hibernating colours beneath snow.

If I am left with nothing but this purse
of sand empty in my hand

If the letters grow into moonlight
and become the small sleepless book of my heart.

Above the letters

Waxing the small feet of the bees
the green thirst watching over us,
the spider's thread stringing the mandolin
on the whaleback of the soul.

Counting the cloves of the shamrocks
we fell from salt heavens with our luckless coin
shinnying into the half sunrises
the brogue of gypsy light.

The sparrows' house concerts,
the left away in the surgery of fallen leaves
the leaping faith of the answerless,
song panning the gold.

There beyond, where only the smallest eye
flies in lurching whispers, above the letters
where all things die into the digging earth
lovers' hands finding their empty lockets.

A blasphemy of colours shyly turned away
on that hill of regret where storytellers gathered
writing in a blood that will not dry,
kinetic odes, on bark paper, washing the chariot burial of the sun.

Funerary of a lagging morning rusting in the draconian white,
the hora of death, skipping deathless
pathless song, place above all others
where love cannot die.

The taste of blue and red

The blue words include I do, I am.

The red words fly above us
within the small reach of our hands

awaiting a Sabbath word that is stoking a fire.
Brother, sister, these are blue words.

Strangers for whom we have no hope,
crucifixion, agony.
These are red words.

Blood is the songstress of red, crêpe paper-thin,
its lullaby of blue carrion
and lovers' moans.

I have lost my work many times
the ever endless understanding of self,
reciting the red words.

I have sold the blue words to a faerie
for a penny tied to my pocket
tangled and buried deep beneath the ground.

When I think of the first wheel
the first fire,
I know there are no beginnings.

These are red words.
You must follow them to the end
of what you know.

Almost blue, almost red.
And what holds you like a colour
in its hands.

The letter green

The poorest of the poor wait there
pass us a ghostwritten song, nested in a parable of rain.

I tell you in every damned cat, the wild love of angels
that shadows down like quiet snow.

Spring's meticulous return, turning the opus page
and the bleating of sheep, mushroomed

like bell shaped stupas, husking the grain-edged light
blanketing the forest with unbelievers' psalms.

A crescent moon finger paints the word
silver-tongued, stealing the girded dragonfly's dance

that itself dwarf tumbles towards the earth, shedding the not-worth-speaking,
the spears of grass where it lunges.

The river, and above it all the night sky, flows through the vein of a leaf
fossils of stars, cretaceous ants in amber, rock sheltered, spider still.

And if all we can do is teach that pleading silence,
hold its voiceless mew, the knot of its loveliness

Remembering the powdered glass opera of that desert psalm
honeyed in that letter green, and what is forever born.

Hermeneutics

To observe yourself observe
the silences kissing the skin.

The most ignoble truth a discus of light
thrown with the might of Olympian lust.

A silk road to the beryl-eyed cliff,
where lemmings cross over and skiffless sing.

In the thimble books of Heraclitus, the thin bones of sparrows,
woodchucks and pond fish in the starlight.

The fragrance of a deepening rainbow furiously born,
the sure oblivion of meaning.

Brightened in the magician's hand
gables of uncreated light, the hermeneutics of a corner painting.

I listened to how yes said no, who could not hear its silence,
the flower sellers' hearts whispering to the shyest flower.

Book chests of beauty, catching silver from the river's belly,
the dressmakers that dressed the poem with song.

A harem of wilting tinselled sonnets
in the sleepless chant of black, too small for the sound of summer's name.

And I leave you with this question, void of the angels and immortality, to listen, more quietly, like a night with no stars.

The

History

of

the

Unknown

World .

The history of the unknown world

Angels come as suffering,
green shoots in Pasternak's garden

the god shout of straw and amethyst,
letters chiselled on Hebrew scrolls.

Music sighs, the hollow of dusk in night,
a handful of shooting stars

on shaman drums
beating clear white light.

It is raining in my eyes
when she says I am leaving

the fugal horn burying the labyrinthian silence
where hermits sing.

We are at the end of the rainbow
every colour but gold.

Song of a flower in bloom

I am a poor prophet
with a song of a flower in bloom.

My neighbour is a henchwoman
who would have my jester's soul.

My lover has heard her tin rattling,
tallow for a wick.

Everywhere there is one soul
waiting on one soul to move astray.

Everywhere two counted from one
a hundred dogs barking its music.

I am by the river where the blind man walks
and the lovers come to see their face in the water.

Before the weather turns I will arrive
lost as never before.

Before I lose my breath
I will become that water.

I am all that is blue, all that is grey
in bloom forever with its song.

The taste of snow

It rained the whole night of the universe
love with its broken wing
praising winter's song.

The angel of the goddess
with her long-stemmed light
tapping on the eavestroughs.

I want to be a gunslinger, a grail knight
a rag merchant for her love,
spice the caverns with thin moons
and half disappearing names.

Lovers with a quill of fire
lean from their balconies
raise their fists in the rain.

With a kindling magic
and a diaspora of silences,
stars drifting into stars.

A paper sadness
by a tin sadness
by the agony of gold.

A sleepless white snow
flies over the world
and all of what we are sleeps on.

Afrikana

Blackness, black as song
black as starlight, black as rain

blackbirds and crows
black doves, black jugglers and the blackest kisses

black letters from the Queen Regina
to her black slaves.

And black the night of the grouse and of the black goose
and the black spring of feathers

the ever after of black heavens
and black wild horses, with black manes.

Black even in emptiness
in the fields of the masters

building the black temple of the black other
in black clay.

Jubal

Secrets, secrets we are given
endless thimbles, ribbons of masks and empty sail.

Brooding symphonies
and a blessed delinquent joy

barn cats and swallows
circling the heart's praising ground.

Whispered, whispered
from the thin eye of the whale

grey agonies and the black tar of a word.
Skies filled with simple arithmetic

hawks and falcons
and the geometries of a wild dove.

Bone spurs of heaven, the language of a cutter's whip
and a higher purpose waiting for its gated light.

Long is its silence and round its worship
climbing high enough for the lover tapping at its thigh.

Fire clouds and breached still hours
turning pages for the village mystic

waiting thrown into the gospel
of waiting.

Mercy with its mercy ships,
the sunset in a lover's eye

a feeble amen and crippled moon
and all is well.

Last angels

for June Callwood (June 2, 1924 – April 14, 2007)

Good and kindly woman
here have I found you, carrying your empty basket.

Scrapbooking the names, the last of the to do's,
the silvering of the branches in your misted hair.

Those haggling smallish hands
that polished the apple of every season

falling in the ripe of your eyes from the highest eves,
an arpeggio of leaping strings

overheard above the hushed fields
of a midsummer's night,

lovers cuddling the narrow green, winged like Puck,
tying their ribbons

to the thin boot of the moon,
the cornflowers singing their names

the music of shy secret gardeners
and cinnamon angels, and the pug nosed world sleeping on.

June, these blue veins like sassafras,
shine on our empty sound

the thin wren of it all grubbing before us
like a salt-licking wound

or speak-easy mice, scurrying from the lime pits
or glory kettles, stars weaving stars.

There you are, dear woman, hand on the loom
of tomorrow's tomorrow,

weaving the rhyme, the humbling ocean sermons
swimming in the guest book of night,

with its twilight Orphic muse, homing there
above the startled flowers, that calm beauty in your eyes.

There's nothing next, you say
the prop root of the bygone, like a weeping scholar's praise,

pruning the dry bones
in the lichen forests chasing one bird, after all.

The pin money of yet another spring, of one last half day
where gods beat us, love us, into one of them.

Rotting wilderness branches,
green regifting green, in another's winter eye.

My good kindly woman
You are almost there.

A raga of sunset, and never ending beginnings
the gifts of last angels, their tireless bribes.

Hold less tightly now,
its clutch of weather and ceaselessly burn.

Falling From the Blue Tree

Falling from the blue tree

for Sarah

It is red, like a small farmer's moon, or tiny suns picnicking there
and so we climb, as if the twine of a loving jig or kitten chasing its peacock's tail.

It is there to reach into, to teach like all things that are love borne
and you ever spirited, eyeing its every movement, and whirling still.

Only to dance in its branches, like any singing bird, or thing with wings
like any tree-whisperer who paints a word they themselves will never understand.

We dream and weave, in that grey remark, the leaves tumbling, each vein
a lock of twilight that has returned from a sweetness it too cannot name.

You will grow larger in the softness of your falling, for you are already nesting there
a frozen moment, already perfect, sun-gliding in that wishful green.

A long way away from this, a mighty song awakes,
a parable in the smallness of my hands, a faerie quietly waiting, on both shores.

And you who see the soundless fire, invisible you will dance,
like every great dancer, trapped within your spine.

An organ grinder's blur of aimless magic glance, clumsy feet begin to move,
in a quiver of scudding dusk, bright arrow that you are.

The blue melon sky, like a music box, grows like that polished light,
into heavens we cannot cleave, a name we mutter into emptiness.

And there, filled with all things alike, a dervish, or lama, or tzaddick,
the wise women, and shamans, priestesses suddenly real.

Cliff sirens in the unspeakable air, angels with golden toothpicks lifting your eyelids,
a blurring wish list that soon you will photograph, spiralling in every living thing.

Blue winter

In winter you ask spring to sing to you, my friend,
The poems we once chased, now chase us.

The speech of owls, and blue winters, in the eye that looks back
And in the dance of daunting ending days, dreaming everything we love at once.

Speaking lost hours to those things that cannot hear, but listen,
The step of faith falls rhapsodically when you are enough of a song.

And though we say death, and mean life, who is speaking, who is listening,
And on what parchment does the miscreant blood dry.

There is a writer of every war, a blanket of running fire that cradles the young
In heaven's adroit history, dromedaries in the genuflections of mind.

You bring with you its hostage, merchants of name, all that is long borne
A wave is a sea, is a seer in the seen, now we have lost our way.

Lakes and the lair of the candlewick, caregivers of water you said,
This is meditation, this is all we have, now swim.

This is one star in the universe, the galaxy is yet an inch away
Kill the word, become the word, be the planet and fly about the universe.

Beneath you there are stars, above you there are pigs with wings
Dwarf suns, and the lending house of joyful wandering, energy, the song of itself singing.

And then it all begins, the negative description chiming the non-linguistic knowing
The unspoken ruffling of the feathers of the most beautiful words.

All signifier and sign, chasing the tail of the other, into a bushfire, bullion of wheat field
Barely a spark between the tongue and the jukebox of tangerine sound.

Lover's hands speak, by the morning glen where the first light is unseen
The whole of what was into what is, scurries into the blue love, and forever after.

Blue music

It's a broken gamble, the reach between touch and the stars
In it the traders arrive with silence enough to be free.

Even when the whale comes by, the old ones worry
They know it is time for summer to be carried into a new way of seeing.

The leaves flee, the hum of winter, and the talk is of food and shelter,
But eyes lust shape and smell in the reflection of the dry stream.

Lovingness is far away, a frieze of aria written by a chiefly angel
Who knits sweaters for the bare trees, white garments they will wear, and melt into.

Thoughts arise like lowlands, seed bearing the sun
Stuffed like scarecrows and the will to frighten winged sounds.

Where all the choirs barter with the same coin, on the same sure-footed gods,
Nattering something about forgiveness and charity,

Rising on the aurulent mercy, that whirligigs above like stalactites,
And the dirty maple that girds a child's eye.

The one who dwells in a cave retells the wine season,
And those thoughts that sting the heart's lonely travellers in the bending of each season.

And in between, that unknown place, where no one is listening,
The remembrance that sires its pennywhistle sadness.

What treachery there is in the arms of the great hurt that is love,
When the earth is wet with our tears, the body that leans into mind.

A twisted oasis of saddened joys, riddled sly, as the witch burning skies
Here is there-is-here turning on the potter's wheel, in the fossil of blue music

Suddenly free, real as splendour, a broken wing, a frail word,
The frond of infinity that pollinates the eternities.

Where runs the Ganges, on the fingertips of lovers, the harmonium of wind,
The blood flame of one after another, swift as a sail of spirit wind.

A garden in each sprouting seed, regatta of the universe,
The birth moment of regal seasons, numerous as time.

Blue before the throne

Once in a blue moon, those yellow birds shout,
the sagely twilight lifts its feet,

a death jar of smooth hours
pawning the silver lining of stars.

Fits and starts of rain waking the earthworms
the pixie in her star-spangled shoes,

the Seer of Lublin, a song from a deaf ear
in a brightened late night howl.

Diasporic odes written on the spine of each leaf
fleeing with the hearsay of Romans and wild berries,

the holy trickster of wanting
that spears the flesh like a warden's silence.

From the margins, the wolfing sounds,
little castles that seize pleasure's wounded sadness,

the stone's thirst above, mortified in kindness
in the delft sky, where that dandy Vermeer wished upon a star.

And nocturnal sweet reveries, like acorns beneath our feet
the pearl of the fingernail moon, in its hoop skirt

dancing about, like a naked David and Assisi
and we, just happen to be awake.

Look further, the juke of the homeless
butterfly wings snaked in the tree of breath,

turning the page of the hereafter, a gnarled infiniteness
the captain of one word, blue before the throne.

A small blue sadness

I love this quilted blue
where everything sings with one eye closed.
The circle of light that chants the unowned,
the lashing of coins that draws its shallow breath
and fills the air with the tiny bones of song.

The thin anointed cloth and crimson anarchies,
the yard books of silence
and wild heath of soul,
bright scarves jangling in the blood
twilight languages curled into a name.

Oh what a word there is for this,
a magnificence burning,
a burqa lifted upon itself.
The moths that stir in the loin
the angel of mystery and a birth-giving dawn.

By the swing bridge of faith
blind colours and famine ships
the sun a flaming instrument
a speechless light
a slave army marches upon.

What kingdom is not unlocked
when lovers kiss.
A small blue sadness unsaddles the foal of sleeping hill
fills the unfilled cups,
a greenish coin in a gilded cage sings

A humming blindness recites
its most beautiful scripture.
The shell of everything broken
whispers the secrets of itself,
and all the world lifted into song.

Stars

Stars

Cinders they are, laughing inmates
circling the fire ants, the wire birds of prey

God light in their bonnets, and flaming tail feathers
chasing a leaf without colour to the pirate stream

Above the honey trees on a thousand hills
their arrowless faith planting their halo of infant light

In the onion fields and painted blue mosque
catcalls of ivory dusk, muezzin from the minarets singing

As they climb like a skirting breeze, rise where lemons ripen
witching the seaward chapel rain, shingles of night,

A covenant of vowels searching the above for an earth-like planet
the clutter of them, a universe wide.

And when one falls, a second ago, a tent of sleepless sky
handling them down, where the buttercups and heather bloom

Over the cypress trees and bread maker's psalms,
the gifts they cannot command, tunelling the illusion we are

Beneath their tutelage, hapless beggars before their little kingdoms,
birth watering the polyphonic unmarked grave.

Every child pulls a red wagon about their forgotten sermon
on celestial love, their valedictories where a slave's hand martyrs gold,

Mimes to behold for the women lepers of Albina,
and the goat herders of Mount Asur, two hundred centuries ago.

They were there, banshees threadbare in shawls of lovers, that stood
helplessly frozen before smaller gods,

Remembering a first kiss, each wanting to stand beneath them forever
fetching the stories, secreting their way,

Touching, only to die beneath the brightened path
cobblestone and ringdoves and rainbows born,

Shams in the desert and the Babylon Ishtar where the dead outnumber the living,
while monks' absolutions birth the answerless height.

By their small droplets of light, the letter trading of blood,
the voiceless table song of the lamb,

And the wild thoughts answering our prayers, lighting the candle,
to face the eternalness of their names, peace be upon them,

Thunderbolts and broken hearts crying out, mending the unknown
in the uncradled darkness when every beloved meets,

Their tiny harp playing the music of the tithing selves, each silence overheard
and we look up and see ourselves at last.

Caravan

I measured the book of stars
I looked in the canyon that is painted red

with a red hand,
and a rope's length of blue, as old as the song of I am.

A spire of paper lanterns, and a circling liquid gold
canaries yellow as daffodils' wings.

Yes, this is the old language,
God's servant pillaring the ants.

The joyride of a wing dancer, in the vineyard of self,
a caravan of flame swallowing names,

heart-trading the parched eye,
each hyacinth lighting the candle of another.

It is on fire there, the crystal muse of loneliness,
a coin falling into the well of the silvered image of itself,

a gilt-edged page with the thinness of love
tea leaves in the slumped over death camp grass.

Slumbering in the overturned burnt tracts
where wide-eyed hens count the lower heavens.

And hells above hells, in each other's eyes
the dove blinds of Dante Alighieri,

counting the fill of emptiness with vows
planting trees in the hoped-for light.

El Camino

for Oliver Schroer (June 18, 1956 – July 3, 2008)

A million stars, Oliver
and when one goes out, the village bell rings,

the sleep in the eye of a golden light that has no story
a treasure chest of white fields and beggars' kisses that fall in the phlox of night.

The mortal compass of our watching hearts
the barrel music that skins the angels,

schooling the starlight
that wrings its hands, and gifts the smallest maps.

The jug band of whistling emptiness
witching the desert manna,

the praise song in the knot of wood that reels in the Stradivarius,
a small white butterfly with green diamonds on its wings.

And Caesar bows when I tell these Corinthian legends,
put my instrument away and sing instead to dying flowers,

the poor hand of a dog-eared wonderment
casting gilded dragons into streams.

And words, those poor visitors
on that long endless path, of saints and stone churches

the smallest part of the whole,
high flown in the darkness of the sea.

Singing in the seashells and tree wood
your fractal reels and forest blue,

and a sleeping homeless star
that holds the empty sound forever.

Equinox

The woodchucks like china dolls
and all about the singing voices

The bee eaters, the fence birds
digging in the light.

The word appeared
I pointed to a star

Shed the silences it said
half-shadowed out of charcoal.

I photographed the moon
stars crooning in their rum and chapel speakeasy

Creaking in their bullying sleep
baying like water chasing a granite shore.

Bringing in the shells that pencil the sea
shutter speed of whippoorwills in the grassed-over wind

And moth wings in every hand
that holds the invisible there.

You are a wand, to wave over yourself
a song falling on its sword

That is itself a god, eggshell white
in a tarred and feathered universe.

Crickets born a millionth year ago
willowing their Sabbath prayer

A peacock fanning the bowstring of tears
murmuring Phaedrus in the long woodland grass.

And that doubled abode of light
the night that creates itself out of nothing.

And only a steeple above the slowly changing ruins
all that cannot be seen.

Blind

Blind they are softly begging, like a silkworm's whisper
softly sing the bucket stars into the night,

Blind, a quiet moon quietly crying,
field stars crashing into a wearied epitaph, old enough to be light.

An unearthed song, blindly tossed into the peg dust of a blind and tiny heart,
and all of your knowing not, growing a seed inside

Lovingly blind, maps folded, sent flying like paper birds
hard of listening like a waif by the stone-edged walls

And you in who have heard so much in so little
blind now, hush, hear how little you are

In the golden thirst of the grass, in the rust of fallen leaves
hear again in the unutterable stutter, muttering come blindly, come.

Blinded when you rise into any coming or going,
a lake of trees or swanning with that gnarled koan,

Wind-paths before birth, when roads were rivers and stars blind lanterns
or simply one or another god.

And there on that narrow bridge that is only ever a word
blind-hearted loathing in the spinning wheel of blindness

Blind is night, and blinder still, the day that sees
in the guild of seeming, light itself.

Blind, become smaller, blind in the telling of blindness
the covenant of a compass rose,

The page close enough to the eyes, at once all of white, and you in it
blind, and then forever blind, cherished, precious, disappeared.

The history of stars

A red tulip, crouched in the Levant of a rising morning,
a nuthatch in the half-mooned birdhouse.

This I dusted from the rusted skylight
shaped as it was like a crowning heart.

I am reading the ever resting long road before me
the bloody-eyed flowers, the fealty of illusion

and the mannequin-like juries, foot-twisted there,
kneeling before jute sacks, and junk stars, asking

in the theatre of moonlight,
with turpentine lamps and whisky hours.

Give me a hatchet, a scythe to bring down
this crawling fragrance, the white dwarfs that shed their skins

like the Manitou spirits in the pebbled stream,
and thimble green nesting places,

the crossroad where crows gather into a hundred Ojibwe names,
and live a thousand lousy years one word at a time.

I am singing still, my leg dragging the iron,
the skin of my brain beaten, like any servant of two masters,

a song maker in the juke joints of danced-about sighs
an infant's crawl of mighty word, surely a final nod.

The little ones, small as humble plants, invisible garlands
in the regilded dress of the silver tattered odes,

apostrophic colours in the black robed light of tailored lakes,
sail red forest and the history of stars.

Love untouchable

I am only dreaming wild magnolias, begin by saying this
Then the magi and the one word that lynches the thorn.

A stream of lust, tiny mobsters in the cowslips,
Fearless songs filled with ocean tides.

The light crazed galaxies turning the weavers' garment black
The goldbeaters that ring upon our sky-bodied heart.

The rose crown that shouts the birth notes
And the rag of stardust regilded as the moth.

And when the moment turns sideways, a watchful eye closes
Netting the open spaces, winking the days away.

The miracle is like this, waxing into the wick of the flame
What holds the moon, the music box where asking is born singing.

Finger running the fields, heartlessly sounding the nectar of the beehives
The red kissing melons conducting the arias of crustacean scribes.

In the lark's chambers lavender and paper flowers like thin clocks
And love, love untouchable, guardian of sun locked angels.

The old evangelist kings, a mountain kneeling in the valley
And David tossing his pebbles into the blue and everlasting night.

An inebriated maestro, falling into earth and heaven alike,
I am dreaming only wild magnolias.

Bell weather

Chase the tails of stars, and rattle the silence,
Gather the weeds, and praise the wild flowers

Wild are we that are tamed, a graceful loss, gracelessly won
Gather thyself in the firmament of falling stars,

The royal light that turns a page
And see in the beheld, the most beautiful of all, the beholder itself.

II

From

the

Book

of

Angels

From the book of angels

I began to grow one wing
and saw myself from above,
eyes sad with the names of the world.

I have slept past midday,
the whip hand frightening the dream,
long orange mane of the sleeping sun.

Oh quiet night where every song is born
in the quicksilver of the unhanded,
chalk-bound in stars, forever climbing.

Above the garden tangled hair,
breathless sighs,
angels feathered black the unspeakable word.

The fruit of painful joy that spears the light
rests upon her eyelids, sleeplessly
and seedless grows.

Regifting the above

to Siovone

Regifting the above, in the slender tail of night
that falls into the stub of the moon.

The clocksmiths in their tavern of stars,
that tap upon the smallest parts to wake the whole.

The twilight hours wrapped in their garment of black,
pinned to the mirror that silvers the spheres

of golden feathered illusion, and disbelief
bird spirits sleepwalking, that climb like long-tongued bees on vine flowers,

the "I and thou" of starfish and morning glories
slumbering through a ghostly winter's snow.

Like lovers who have slept through their own words
unrobed to their elbows, sweetening the allegories.

And to what they most distrust must pray,
chanting the cotton verse, wingless above the wind.

Homer's arrows blooming light,
the Greek gods lifting banners to the oracle

spidered into the death wish of rainbows,
only to have known how far from near is born.

The hornets that follow the flesh into word,
worry beads that count gently beneath the breath,

As gently you have come, to whisper the life of a village dream,
unfolding in the circumference of red,

the origami of a faithless, nameless wage,
bone white, the blood running dry.

And even as I hold that flame stone beneath my tongue,
and feel again the grail of trading light, for a moment, grow old,

lost in the long beauty, inseparable, stumble-footed
I watch my words hand-singing,

This ventriloquy of sadness that holds the night hostage,
God comes but once, and lovers a thousand times.

And yet that curve that holds the breath upon your shoulder
is my tongue, now only beginning to speak, while so quietly you dance.

And I watch, like one who watches the dying of a season,
though I am the light, and the tree and the fire that will burn it slowly down.

Church stone

We ran like birds in the night
triangles for wings in the corn tails

black darters, the common moorhen
on the rail of moonlight.

The little broken and stepped on daisy
in the cutout well of hidden flowers

the hallelujah singers in the beaten temples
in the chanting rooms of the wild iris,

its zebra striped underbelly coved in the great marsh,
the small bride lists in the covered booth,

secrets like church stone
deepening in the fields.

The candle flame of moth and dragon wings,
the mimicry of the orchid,

an empty glass slipper,
green and forgetful and renewed.

The history of leaves

Three divine kisses
chaperone the orphaned kindnesses.

The quiet miracles cuddling her thin shoulder
the small dovish shadows that cry out no name.

The sermon of lovers in that monkish red oak
two little chestnuts entwined on that abandoned hill.

And all about the jewelled-like sounds
the trembling word that dies on the lips of the sea.

The scrap song that prepares the table before our enemies
where pointing angels have fallen.

For a beggar's harp, the whole of my soul
in the same singing reed, dying into green.

The arrow in your own heart,
the curfews in that thimble of praise.

And lovers who open their arms into the wineskin
of rain boots and fallen trees.

The sun is my own she sings, that golden lance,
I will trade you brimstone for a camel's thirst,

Your eyes are my eyes, swollen shut with honey,
song maker of the thin jute of the world.

Love, is to know the enemy in thyself
that lock of hair, that brings the heavens down.

In the council above, the hidden books
empty sacks of knowledge, praising the smallest things.

Broken teacups, the opera of fiddler crabs, a death camp orchestra,
and the history of leaves.

Spider's thread

I gave my love a sweetheart pin
whispering which mountain more holy than any other.

From a spider's thread each diaphanous name,
ruffling its feathers in the inkwell of night.

In the meadow phlox, the jeweller's art of dying moments
the Greek flame in the parable of her hair.

The date syrup and rose water, chanting the mantra of music criers
lovingly gardening the blue Jacaranda in full bloom.

The praise song of red in the sumac
white elms unfinished in the word.

Candy flossed, carved in the inhospitable glories,
flocks of wings covered in snow.

One book will ask for another, the taxonomy of each silent letter,
dying into itself, a harem of light, of love.

Kissing the white

Each carves its unspeakable love
the ground birds awakening husks of sacred thread.

Spring reciting itself to an unfaithful lover
tracing the thin of the softest quiet,

the circus morning that brings through town
jugglers with their feathery hats.

Elephant-faced gods, red as an angry night
and the coiled cheeks of the children, who dance like rain.

Rings of bright and brighter,
the crucified myth tumbling between them.

Something finds us in that homelessness
that shallows down,

the grail of a snailing wind blinding soldiers
bottlenecked in the rootless white night of sorrow.

I painted your breasts when you slept
the living tiniest moment glittered, flooding the mountain paths,

lifting the sun, buttoning our eyes, the garment
that falls into nakedness.

Like drifting clouds the world mouthed
the dust born sparrow fluttering in the church grass,

in the hour of bones, the curling spine
curtaining the leaves, enchanted the suffering made whole.

In the gypsy cave, you dress like Kurdish waters
and in that cove in the north of Spain you were quiet

as the Spanish conquistadors closing the book of the sea
or a chapel mouse in the plain dustbowl fields, that revels its hymn.

The topping of trees, vast emptied chalices
workers' hands like estuaries, in the roof wood

the dockworkers foot-stomping
the ragtail improvisation of love.

Toy wands and star fruit, a symphony of timeless villages,
how little I remember.

Kissing the white orchid roundness of her belly
Sarah in the desert, birthing the wordless stars.

Her maidservant stringing a wandering thirst
like rose boxes, ribbed in the heat of the day.

The charcoal maker with no name
and a wildness untying those robeless letters,

whispering algorithms of the soul, bottomless rivers
and a music that keeps on playing.

In Tangier

Learn to tell me about you
your lips like a pumice stone

that marks the moon as
shining simply there.

And your hand a choir of red
a slave's hand, dreaming backwards

A journey homelessly arriving
when you sing this way so quietly.

The tiny streets of your heart, lynched in the Kasbah
twinned with sea froth and the grace note of longing.

A rude silence lifted from your tongue
hanging from a length of rope, lightly in the air

Like a gallows, and what moans in the night
a thousand feet below.

Only the maps change

Only the maps change, I said, and meant her body,
the glow of the fig in the orchard of her eye.

The sugar kiss melons cauterized, caught in the night grass
honey coloured sacks, gravity bound by touch alone.

A trail of Cossack's blood on the wild stallion wind
the braille of every lover's hand, ropewalking the chains.

The history of all of human striving, the agape moon endlessly arriving
the heart that beats the war drum, in its lovestruck ear.

The same hand that builds the chariot cities, on templed hills
and the white copper stars, asterisks of light.

The wedding music of birds, marooned under a paper mache sky
a soft note turning, perched in a mother's fable.

In the pit and gallow of hours, the prayer to end all prayer,
grey scaling the palace throne.

I hear the gavel, the hounded scents,
red streaks of cloistered hope in the pomegranate's lust.

Stay close to your happiness, for it is not your own,
all of spring in the wasteland of its winter abode.

Long-hearted beats whispering sweet nothings, in the shelter of sea
colour pencilling the hidden coves ghost ships pass by.

Lovely

Lovely the name of One
manhandling a papered moonless night

the sound walk of morning stars, and lovely too,
the old language that mounts the invisible nag.

A song too is lovely my love
and the small feet of spiders

lifted above a god or goddess
that shines a coin for the beggar who wishes it almost into being.

In the counting house, with gouged-out eyes
the smallest things watching over us

with the hand grinding stone carving biblical emptiness
too vast for the word, and seeing in it, the believed.

Lovely the tears in the opera of a lover's eyes,
a glacier calving into a sea

and the small Buddha cat wild and urgently calm,
wise as Solomon, in his lotus bow.

Victorious the cattails creating out of moonlight
curtaining sand dunes hidden in glass,

Loveliest of all, how it sings in all things
and grows from above below.

The life of a single word

In the garden she bends, in her peasant dress,
by the patch of wild daisies

gaunt as baby's breath, a shield of ghostly white granite
a burlesque of early waking stars.

I watch the portraiture, the curving silhouette fading
the clay with its potter's wheel imitating art

errata of the gods, in the wiles of me,
a wounded constellation unkempt in her hair.

I unfolded the perfect origami of the unmapped universe
and was her warrior, her hunter, the stillness of a bowman's hand.

I knew she would disappear into a night that would not end
I knew a shepherd would come to take her silence away.

Love is the religion of morning doves, riddles sleeping by rivers,
where a princess awaits her own heart.

Wherever you are I am, I wrote
and then crossed it out, knowing its plagiary.

There are words so beautiful, they are not meant to be spoken
yellow sunflowers so incoherently perfect, no poet can paint,

That perplex, even the mind banished from mind
blooming in every wild flower, a celestial command.

You are there in the cherished teaching
where sadnesses wander like saddhus, oaken tall.

The poetry of Isaiah's fire, the cadres that would not sleep
the warrior on both sides of the battle.

I promised her nothing more than to stay alive
she asked for what all lovers ask, the beginning again.

Would not have I died for the life a single word,
did I not taste the travelling honey, that wheeling cloud of Buddha's heart.

One eye is blind, tired of the driftwood shaped like a freshly cut flower
the other faithless like field stone, each one more beautiful than before.

What disappears

for Isabelle

What disappears in me is the wisp of your shoulders
and the psalm books with their rain.

The white butterfly that lifts my eyes to the highest wound
the yoke and sail of love's quiet chance.

The highest bow blessed, black sonnets tied to the pier,
in the candelabras of a wooden night.

The sun rises with its one hundred thousand prophets,
what moves on cutters' fields and grazes upon the yellow tail grass.

What sings the unbearable joy,
disguised as swaying hills and wild-eyed death.

A shepherd's stool in the sparrows' trading fields
the bards who wed verse with their hands.

Oh lamb burning, the secret names of the world,
parachute of small petals, and the long feathered touch of our eyes.

Omniscient is she who lifts her body into song,
what threads a blue spinning wheel, that bends a lion's jaw.

Netting the strings, a quill of sleeping shadow
that angelizes the narrow bridge.

A goldenness that leans into a blind hereafter,
when shoemakers closes their eyes.

What disappears in me is that very wish, to drink the nectar
be still, and return our promised land.

Chagall's garden

The mice blind in Chagall's garden and the nightwatch, with its widowhood of hours, droves of scarlet letters and a dowry of starlight tapping the strings of love.

In the light of the well, the bell ringer streaming the word to see itself through another's eyes, a caravan of tiny kingdoms, homages to the small chapels of the dark-throated swans. Riddled in the air, I ask for your hand and flood hymns are given, straying silver odes in a hask of stars.

This is how it was when I wrote my night letters on the sleigh backs of tin whistles, where we lay down in the shadow of nothing, hill stars wandering into absinthe and the black candled skin of Salome. The early twilight, faint as a rose, yellow jackets in the out-of-body wilderness and the young Keats in his penny-grave like a Bedouin singer, cats' eyes in the hourglass of Rome.

The chalice of honey wine, raptors shedding angelskin, vesper birds from the wet camps, frail winter flowers ribbon-like in a turn of chance. The treasure wagons filled with love's slender hands, the drumhead and bow lute, trumpet vines and ragas that bend all the amorphous constellations, shells of the humble-footed fleeting gods.

By the river house stories are told. The cacti watering sea flowers, the ram sacrifice rigging the sky, the view box of Critius, and a candle against the moon koan, decoding the books of the sea.

It is night, always night, the grass dance of the kraal of the universe, the hushed sound of grappling hooks, basket weaving the texts of love, the tinkers with their callipers, measuring the width of one word.

I drank from the wind that lovingly filled the cup, the jiin of the cotton fields and the conch of the sea. Here the goat herder, the beggars dressed like Odysseus, sitting by the vale of the everlasting, the tractate of a single flower, and the letter's waxed seal.

In the Lubyanka, the cello cries to its master, which parable binds us to which rubaiyat of light. A patchwork of hummingbird wings, windmills tilting to patternless sounds. Tsvetaeva, the black swan of perishable knowledge, in the teal of the morning after.

The wooden skids, the crates of white gold, lifting the tortoise-shell dawn. Tusks of floating string, elegant kite song, the hook of night, hand over hand, the crossover wand that births the birthless grey.

Now, in the liquid blue palace, the swaddling cloth of Babylon, god thirst chiselled on the heart of a tree. There I met my angel, a house wren like glass, the script teller laughing, your red mittens sleeved to the runes of my nakedness. The shoeless one making a coat of winter, and from the stone hut, the flickering happiness the softness of white.

I remember the fleece of it, a blue-tailed damselfly speaking in whispers, the hunter gathering a wicket of names. Oh how I wanted your body, how I chant-tuned the bone flute, the music that conquered the hills. The shaman drums, a chorus of nightingales and the long hand of the bells, twitching mannequins, the paparazzi that followed us into the killing fields.

The lovers' letters live on, black fire on white, the brightened star path of it all. What is this dance that waits all night, in animal skins, whittling on soapstone, in the middle of time, filling papyrus, bowing to the Tao of the earth, sinless, a phalanx of slow-eyed madness.

Now I must sing alone.

The
Metafictions
of
Om

The metafictions of Om

A moon perched over a field is much
And a flock of lost stars coming home

A simple drop of dew, and the tiniest winged thing,
Writes all the books when the eye closes on itself

In the invisibilities one silence wrestling another,
The thin diaphanous birth cry of Om.

In my lifetime I knew many things
But when I died I learned this

The configuration of rattling sabres quieted
Gardening in the rainbow of the dervish whirling

And all the Tao of words glitter where only a waggish tail
Smells a thousand fragrances

And on the tuning fork of a blade of grass
The last and first breath make love.

Forever listening

When God said Om, man became a bird
The Navajo know this, and the Cree, the Sky Father who remembers the names of the river
When Adam first craved the dust that has no trembling and fear
He knelt by the stolen fire, this syllable cradled in its arms

On that day Eve fell like a rainbow from an ashen sky
A splinter in the colouring book of no names
A green sprout heel-clicking, beneath the sonorous winter,
The golden crowns of the dandelions, the Mother Ganga in the pure ice of the wild blue grass

Hanuman in the gnarled crabapple's crippled heart, note-bending the stars
The coral peach eddies, the early blooming flowers, bent like forest wanderers
Pollinating the purposeless resplendent order, of no words, saintly at last
That ellipsis of song that every poet knows so well, a doting cherub eyeing its child-likeness

Om is that sound breaking the white, painting the boneyard blues,
Busking negro spirituals in the chirr of old shtetl songs
In the farmhouse, the ghosted floor of the summer kitchen, darning superstitions
Sun-smiling, everything in its perplexity, rising at once

Love is that invitation, we say, the wind filling its sail
At nights when I cannot breathe, it breathes me,
And the stars pocketed in the honeysuckle, the sweetness of Om,
That singes the wingspan of night

We watch them fall, some say dance, in the mind of immortal moonlight
Chanting saintly, the eulogy of immolated moths
If now there is a creaking in my soul, it is only that opening hushed
When it shatters the grating silence, forever listening.

Unfolding the rose

By your hand was I made
By your voice was I made silent

By the rales of the tavern scholars
Were words made words again

To know my way home,
I brought you an eastern prayer

On the doorstep I left a glowering rose
Wild frankincense, errands of light

Night is everywhere, kissing the ground
The church and steeple of two tiny hands

A ring on every finger, I am given this dowry
The small mercies that bind my arms to my heart

The czars of hills and slumber weed,
Rubies and pearls, baskets of silken wings

Silver goblets and snow geese in the reed beds
Shy like hunched over lilies, and all of it sleeping

The heavens brought down into our everyday hearts
Unearthed in these rag dolls, the streetlamp blooms

The last of the day, exploding into the quietest colours
Unfolding the rose.

The wine abundant

When I long for you, it is this way
an unheard rustling in the hamlets,

book hawking the warren of roses,
dark circles beneath the eyes of the sun.

Adorned with a more foolish word, handwritten
by an infallible quarrelling,

finger spelling the haunted spaces,
the wine abundant in the ditch wood where the black tulips grow.

The white parchment where a word passes on,
weightless and without unquiet,

our bodies unfolding, as otherness
our hearts silent as weeds.

The beauty that I drank like hemlock in my long sleep,
gently listening, a hedge grove of lovely prayer,

knowing too, no star is lost amongst any other
a dove or swan, swimming everywhere.

I am with Magdalene in the sirocco of
those running wild hearted parables,

the poet warriors with their tired pamphlets
on the feeble heresy of love.

I remember the miracle this way
the shape of the water that swallows the impossible name

and in every way this ribbon of a thousand songs
in the mirror of an empty field, haloed into nothing at all.

The most splendid and beautiful rhyme
that sings in its hollow places, battalions of unending stars

a mystery religion, without mystery
what is ever old, and leaves its silence behind.

Hafiz

The beloved comes. Look he is in her hair.
On the head of a silver pin the seed grain of every scroll.

In the nook of a golden horsed twilight, every rogue sound,
Handwritten in the husk of the season that says 'I am'.

You have lived the word, tied to the doorpost the contest of song
The heir apparent of the true singer of the gosling of light.

In the east heavens, a jewelled illusion chants amen
Skullcapped in a great plume of emptiness.

Hafiz hitchhikes on a cricket of white moths and falling doves,
Shop talkers in that rattle of cradled night.

One second then, the sea draws the sea
I see her singing herself to sleep.

The writers of heavens put their feather pens down,
Ear to the conch shells.

The phantom limb of suffering finger-painting
The calligraphy of love.

I see all of speech as a refutable quote,
All of language a silence not yet silent.

Is there a holy place for anywhere at all, an inch not yet found
A ship lost amongst the splinter of the drunken talk of sailors.

This is not poetry, this is not prose
When the sea raises its dead, upon a floating leaf,

In the dew of a morning not yet arrived
I will surprise myself with my own words, Hafiz,

Though I will have turned to Elysian dust
Singing beneath the leaf its syllabus of common stars.

After Rumi

Call this the loveliness, the amethyst in the angel tree
halo of that poorest twilight on that slope of hill.

The still life of a book where lovers slow dance,
an inch above the soundless wings on their shoulders.

Is it not a song, not to sing. And is it not anywhere, that everywhere appears
colouring the fleeing tunes, the voiceless perfect sunlit bowl.

The cowslips with their eyes closed, gossiping about nothing at all
in our weeping ear, hearing by wondering.

Who am I to solve the tempting cry of all of mind
when the heart opens like winter tulips, swans in their Sunday clothes.

And you, a grainy picture of wishless thinking sounds,
that has died a thousand deaths before.

Christ knows these secrets, the endless of the other side of the world,
returning its sleeping hand.

In the attic room with this aching triumphant pride
humbled to the vision of a sparrow.

One day I am that wordsmith by the pool of the bathing gods
rejigging the one word never before heard

And the next, that beggar with sadness enough to feed the world
a halo of wings, a penny song for your love.

Let the clouds go by, a palace of death,
a clowning bucket wish to fill a yellowed dawn.

Ten thousand musicians with their golden harps housebound
praying to anything green.

Let the singer be a painter and the dancer a painter of words
and in circles meet the same span of leprous tide.

The grains of sand that hear the sea wheat grow
that empty beach where spiralling shells call us home.

Tithing the moments

I kissed the money and ran to the field
with the half-eaten birds

I kissed the fields
their wire eyelids, and drumming little gods

poaching the quail's eggs tinier than silken blue,
candle lighting the word-givers,

crab pots of moonshine, that run down the costumed noise,
wandering into the eye of the unseen.

Smiling like that tall Arab morning
that shoots its strong eyes about the world

like the sly footwork of old monks
spiralling into lilac petals, and the still uneven grass.

Come in my father, my father said
the streets are paved with gold,

each fern, each typhoid spring
each rootless unwashed limb carving a prayer staff.

In the late of day the tiger lilies grow into the theatre of night
the puppet master splaying their rusted yellow leaves

dark orphans in the rabbit holes of ragweed, darting about
the tilting moments, the cochlea of the unsung,

ragamuffin dolls, dancing purposelessly
in the crooked meadows,

Jerusalem in the sunflowers,
the prisoner singing each day before bread.

The forest, with suffering and impish psalms
tithing the moments, stretching the sum of me.

A god in the fallenness of every leaf
the roots taller than the tree.

Isaiah

It is a short book
with its donkey cart of roguish costumed words

written in the mortar of the leaves
and in the din of thinking mind.

It is written on a single petal, and autumn's torn sleeve
on a thistle in the cove of a golden eared river.

In the milk of the cloistered rose, it spells the feathered high air
a tininess watching itself, spice tinkering with throne angels,

a sequin to take back the breastplate of the vesper of love,
the yarn of a thinning spirit unwinding the sloping sun.

It is written in the garden stars,
and thin scrolls that reach about us

the knotted, wailing hands of lovers
the hegemony of tongue and genitals, and grail of fire.

A paradiso of lips, aqueduct of breath pollinating the starless belly
the curds and honey of mirth and legend.

It is written in the back streets of Elysium,
silver bright on the stems of triangular flowers,

long pipes of dusk in the heel of moonshine, and coral shoelace
that steps like a cat over the haggling noise of the city.

Cadences rise into sleeping cornstalks, centuries before
the crematoria, where mysteriously god is named.

A sparrow falls out of the sky, the yellow cake, shadow ash of angels
fanning the bright tail feathers, a crying wind in the manger of night

Valleys and mountains collapse in the high air,
a scripture of smallish talons and bone.

And there looking behind its shoulder, a wheel of white glacial clover,
fields of black sheep, quietly raging.

In the conch of the suffering servant,
the grandeur of an unfinished word, orphaned by deafness

Seeing, hearing, loving, it is written, roaming arrows of light,
the fall of the beginning, long after its name.

Catching silver

You are already that magician in the desert,
red berries falling from your hand

The mystic chanting
one plus one equals one.

Sword makers hollowed into steel
on the anvil of their deepest prayer

Scudding in the returning winds
incurable hearts, cheek to the blade.

How the stars line up in dancer's pose
the eye the mouth the ear

Prayer flowers curiously open and close,
holograms of morning and night.

The one who sang promise in that night without image
and what hulking figure is born

And god, with no name
in the starless love affair that reveals nothing.

Dovesellers

I remember its song
its night of broken glass
when the chalice was wooden
and one blind dove became its scribe.

Desire with its paper boats came
cut its monkish lip
scripture filled its shattered heart
a feather fell against its weight.

Firewands and sermon lit up its beggar's sky.
The hymns of river sickness and moon blindness
the trick song evangelists sing
the braille of history
the hill song that stings the eye.

Fear bled away its autumn light
wild dogs and crows
nested in the hundred and one names of god.
Lions and wolves and lamb song dressed the soul.

Caesar crossed the flood
with its black flag burning.
Faith lists and show trials strirred its ashes,
carried Jehovah into battle
in caskets of gold.

A gospel of bright moons and broken sextons
threw its voice into idols
and beat the drum in its valley of psalms.
Set aflame the secret garden of its names.
The manna of its broken heart
striped upon its back.

Nicodemus in a shoreless night.

Slow moving in the thicket
the pantomime of nations
drunken boats and glass hills of silence,
beauty spinning its veils.

The sabre rattling
of the Lost Book of War and the Song of Lamac
the Flower Palace and Palace of Jewels
in Tarshish and Nineveh
and the Book of Numbers.

The children of the conquered
and the children of the conquerors
shouting down its name.

From

the

Book

of

Imaginary

Letters

From the book of imaginary letters

for Rosalynn Carter

May I waltz with you so quietly, first lady,
night blindness in the small of our own hands.

Crayoned into blue centipedes in the skylight
the old moonshine shackling the thorn flowers.

A glitter of froth and golden cups, that elope with the tuft of unevenness
stardust and three small cockles in a pocket of gold.

That nomadic song that hangs over the magenta of tree angels
and blackbirds' hymns.

Only these monotonous colours without an eye
only the trolley cars and finger snap of street dust.

And the clay-bloodied figurines in the cherry blossoms
the please and-thank-you's of Buddhas born.

What of that moonlight on the cross,
the singsong of vainglorious colors, the handwork of the tallest sounds.

Rosalynn, it is snowing, spores of note-takers, cutting the umbilicus
of thought, half committed to liberty, chaperoning the ever after.

Geese gander in their church-like chariots, each on a summer's night
gossiping of Solomon's thousand wives.

In Tahrir, and Sid Bouzid, the shelter dogs cry out,
the green guide, mute in the heart of the shipyard.

Each hibernating word candling the night,
waterwheels, water clock, and a fiddler's unsigned prayer.

Songs carry us over one another, posses of wonder and awe,
in the butter chatter of frost I clasp my hands, a moon away iguanas close their eyes.

A rag seller's yarn keeps me awake,
burs of light, a scrap of cloth, a thread in the high pasture of green.

I call out each doing, each asking psalm,
high leashed feasts and seas are born,

Small things that fall from the music box,
stray cats on the apron of the moon's gate.

A bowing shirk, the grain grey of your hair, old Baptist ma'am,
and the courage of the poorest among us to say 'I am'.

How did I come upon you, dreaming in the last days on earth
wildly lovelier than girlish charms.

Glory hymns that snatch a libertine's straying eye,
stumbling with nothing more than a palsied word.

An hour moved this way forever,
lorries, amulets, many lovers' voices (these I remember calling from the eves).

And when I am gone, dear Lady, please remember this name
for in all my days I was never less gifted or more uneventfully afraid.

Ear to the sweet tumbling, that is calling me home
from the book of imaginary letters, hushed in its basket of song.

Arab Spring

In that agora of still life
that stirs the cargo of poor heartedness, it begins.

Flame throwers in a quieted breeze
paper swans on a river of blood.

Bits of fallen purpose immolated in the kindle fire,
infinite wisdoms swallowing the infant sun.

The untouchable notes that swagger with moths,
in the crippled wings a red apocalypse flocked in that spark.

Don't forget them when the music lifts the lanterns
and the rose scents reach your ears.

Like a hungry ghost in the dance away of the smaller ones
and the blackface of the dove.

Into that faraway, the street vendor pliéing a motherless night,
the muse in the book house of the heart.

Husking secrets from the shut eye of grain ships
the spider's thread of moon song, from the palace garden.

I carry this overheard silence, shackled to the ordinary stories
faeries and sylphs, and on fingertips the pale of the Arab Spring.

Clenched in the fist of lovers, buried beneath the almond grove
in the golden softness of leaves and forget-me-nots.

Let them tear the world apart, one poor soul at a time
scrolled in Lear's madness, the chrysalis of Caesar.

Sit wherever you are, wherever you may be,
cradled in starlight and tree roses.

The earth with its morning flower opening,
May you want.

Sadr City

The fruit of Baghdad fell
sheathes of bone, locus fire, the quiet of cracking sculls.

The carcass butchers know, this gentled smell that swells
into the dried sea of red.

The small house that tears down the choir of sky
upon it, hallelujahs in every child's mouth.

There are words for the pearls of this,
the small onion path that sails on beneath the earth.

The speech box of love, that toils in scripture
the grass shouting ever greener on every side.

A flag ceremony, of limbs, and a stone cut of eyes,
a shepherd's stool between them.

The bell rings, and only the smoke that lifts the muezzin's cry,
small deaf birds thin as the curling sound.

The ghostly mothers that wander the streets,
in a dusting gulag of light, painted lightly on the early pallette of morning,

The shallow grave of sun, a slave to the night below,
where everything sings unborn.

Tahrir Square

for Abdul Qasim al Shabi

In Tahrir Square they sing a hundred year old poem
Those who fill of night and wish upon a flower.

A thousand other sufferings come out to drink the dew
A thousand cello red stars, that feast upon the sun.

In the stalls of the river vendor that clinch the low ear of the Nile
The raised brow of blessedness, the ancient lyre of rich then poor.

Your palms are soaked with blood...he says,
Lover of darkness, Enemy of light.

Who will give and who will receive are the same
Lovers sigh and ever so small, refuse with their limbs to open their eyes.

The books are burned. Only the words remain.
A vanguard of love, always of love, mirrorless, chanting, nearing no end.

If I say that I love you, the world must bend
As a rainbow, and the last day will go on forever.

In every broken eye, in every broken land
I sail my heart into this freedom.

Yes it is every morning and in every grey ash dusk crowned
He who grows thorns reaps wounds, he whispers,

I watered the heart of the earth,
I soaked it with tears until it was blood.

It is in every glance returned, and in every coin refused
Oh selfish prisoner of the brightened solitudes.

This knotted, wailing hunger, Oh Circus Maximus,
To feel of suddenness, what slowly passes on.

Saladin's glitter of moon with the wingspan of a thousand clouds
Count them out loud, let them be Buddhas, let them be Angels.

It is the Sabbath night of the West
Silver screen and decorum that swan into the afterlife.

Who knows what stories salamanders tell or the fur on the belly of the moth,
Who knows what is untold and told again, written longhand with a spear of grass.

But this thing, this thing that is unholy,
That whisper that cannot be heard, gives back what I am.

Don't be fooled by the spring, he says, *the river of blood will sweep you away.*
And swiftly, I add, our deaf hearts too, in that dull roar of thunder.

The quilt

for Paul Raina

Spring is gone, the flowers spinning still
the Darwinian clocks sprung back to the dreamer.

The winter ends, songs of Odysseus,
in the wake of a lover's ailing hands.

The wraith of a midnight sun, hollow wings
that fell like manna, as my oldest friend died.

A tinsmith bends the heart, the verdict of a gaping sound
a flapping star brooms the earth away.

A shale of muddy waters clears its throat,
hushed oaks and a tusk of tiny whispers solider on.

All of it lunges into the rally of knots
a sentient thinness that cleaves one soul's repair.

No, this is too easy, his spitting blood and cutout veins
the hooligan spring torn from his belly, like a butchered dove.

And my own slow death, the sputum of wind,
the rope trick of seeing all things at once.

Castes of sunsets blooming on the village fool
the wagon-train theatre of clouds, circling I pray.

The quilt of sand that stretches though the green
and his ghost, casting perfect stones in empty fields.

Calendar days

Monday offers a wagtail of songs, and stars shaped like shrapnel in a child's eye.
Tuesday, peonies with honey ants, and divas who sing from buttonholes
Shades of turquoise that bruise the sky, and lapis lazuli,
The slenderest red, hazel and indigo, colourless pinwheels from above.
Wednesday, who cares about Wednesdays, its crooked oaths
It only mutters the poor are wealthy and the wealthy poor,
Thursday is the Sabbath of fisherwomen and midwives
Pick up a stone, the dust of a butterfly wing, toss it into the crest of a wave, a still brook,
A quiet meadow, forever perfectly the heart, a drum that beats in war and peace the same.
Friday is the day of priests, and the seaward whistling in a blade of grass and the downtrodden,
It liked the sincerity of your words, building its tent beneath them
The starlight that lifts its eye in the crawlspace, hawks and doves and symbols of the unseen
Falling into something we cannot hear, but know, by the softness of our fingertips,
Saturday is for the morning dew, the hammer complaining to the anvil
and a black sheep coming home
Sunday asks how does an angel earn its innocence, where do the homeless sleep, the love notes
disappear and those without food, and love, die.

Eulogy

for Zaira

There are clocks in the mountains, winding the glade of emptiness
and music even the shepherd cannot play,

In the songbook of death,
the whispering river orchards and shade trees melodiously chant.

Beneath them young lovers lie, a Blakean insignificance,
whirlybirds caught in a sail of wind, a palsied endless sigh

The curse of each peasant, or the pheasant's splay of colours,
where rainbows quarrel with their Dantean plume.

And now and then, an heir to those saintly shadows arrives
a moment that lasted a lifetime, sparks from a higher place.

Words only words, skilfully enjoined, frayed at the elbows
and the element of the sun, a berm of earth between two shores.

And you old Italian marm, soft angelical mother of cherubs, whom I loved so much,
dreaming each thing asleep and awake,

I know where you rest, where I hold my last breath,
or can I say from your heart my own,

Calked in your son's malthusian eyes,
who held shadow, kindly now in your gentle arms.

If there is nothing to say at all, let me say it well,
nothing ever lost, so fiercely, in that glance of here and gone.

Silences as high as kites drift away in a mother's eyes,
children forever chasing the strings that colour the sky, forever beyond their grasp.

In Calabria, I too was a goat herder, a thief and the one who slept
with gold beneath his mattress, writing on the palm of another's hand

And learned the owl's heavenly ears, the farsightedness of a lotus flower,
its hearing blooming in mud, as we are light, and light-footed.

Only this long pause, this unknowness, that sang so very quietly,
small enough that I might die with you,

And you mother of many,
mightily ruled an empire none of us can name.

The music of tiny hands

In your little years, the shores rang out their stories
Of tinseled flowers and Buddha white angels.

In the wishless thinking it grew
The cowslips blue in the laddered green air.

Listening by the shoreline I can hear the face of silence
Trumpeter swans whispering the small heights of sadness,

A fondness for the starlight and sad piping notes
Threading the music of tiny hands.

The letters of lovers who have never met
The laced scarlet piled like a chalice of autumn leaves.

Mewing in the love songs, corralled in our eyes,
Falling from that ever half sky.

Suns passing suns, dove born stars
That old tamarind intoxicated as a fallen sparrow.

Long in the arms of the moonrise
Nothing is as it seems, so they told their lies.

The little ones with wings appeared
Well praised, and so go on a little while further.

As
the
Black
Rose
Sings

Caravanserai

I could be lost in your eyes forever.
That is the way the old poets talked
to their fevered birds. The sunlit clutch of hills
and the Cerulean singers that pressed themselves
thin against the puffed out sky.

The words are gathered like song
forgetful of their crustacean birth,
the glacial light that fled the sea and left the mountains
in their path. The spinning high shadow, the moonlit scripture
that fled the hills of Rome.

Here a leaf is freed and talkative as the soul.
Here Caesar's world, far away as beginning is end.
The still point, the caravanserai of the body
where ships pass in a lover's eyes.
What prize is there but that ruinous night. And wait there.

Until the gods come down and lead us into their tethered air
and cleave among us the broken things.
The things that cannot be changed or left unchanged,
and gather us there, as if we were a kiss that lasts forever.

The intellect of hills

They have no desire, knowing they obscure mountains and suns
thin against the entanglement of wondering meanings,

Impossible Buddhas drawn into the tangle of unknowable light
that birthed the tumultuous emptiness of stone.

Lovers lie upon their leather stretched skin, leave no print upon their muted bodies
spiralling into the nocturnal thunders,

And with their constellation of hands, stubs of finger and mane of human colour,
dream the tango of childlike touching.

They are mightier than the Mujahedeen and the Meccan tribes who named them,
or fabled winged charioteers who watched the divine battle below,

Where smallish kingdoms bloomed a ghosting vapour of mind,
gorged-out eyes catnapping in the season of their uprising.

Many climb their backs to greet their white-edged underbelly,
the crag of a death mask, hawking their draconian sun,

Then let us lift their veils, the clouds that cover their face like an ancient word,
fleece-like and feather weighted against what cannot be found or lost in their open hands.

And in their eyeless night, cut glass ground opacities, torn perfections
girding their breathless beaten song,

A sailor's plumed sky, a rag of wanderlust, as everywhere they dance
carrying a palanquin of young stars, feasting on nothing at all, certain of their hour.

The ecology of mosquitoes

There is a white horse in their bulbous eyes, a tidal bore,
hunting in the oaken garden theatre

A rogue wave gathering the stilt roots of red mangrove
ghostly red hibiscus dripping the antonyms of a solemn green.

The milken teeth of untamed skylines, summon the theomorphic inferno,
flame songs burning a magical wheelhouse, mingle in their slacked jaws.

No eulogy for their midge like wings swarming in the honeyed scum of starlight,
treading thin air, sea-like, weightless, hovering between snarling silences,

Scrambling sheathes of tiny shrapnel on leaf axils,
or puddles, breeding invisibly in red plastic buckets and flower dishes,

Vectors bright with sutras of suffering prose, spreading disease as the awakened ones did love,
the wet back of small meadow flowers, small mercies and hill poems that brim in the eves.

It is their gift that they are compared to mightiness, the litmus of monolithic prayer,
in the great enterprise of gods, theological questions of why they are here at all

Lingering in motes of daylight, mongering philosopher and cretin alike,
they are our own untold stories, haggard smiles, and illuminati of bitter romance.

Our lovers, and the room between any two bodies removed, unfolded at last
calling out amongst the infinite Cretaceous moons, what only moves this still,

Expanding at the edge of the universe, as they wait, perfectly matched
seeding an ecology of flight, pure as the koan they are.

Hamlet

A black hole in the galaxies is Hamlet's heart,
a fleece of crooked moon and rag book of names

chalked in needle flowers and sunless death,
blind tumbling weed, king of itself.

A lover's thirst that sang in the mud its uncountable star,
wined before the burning lamps its singing bones,

by a candle's light made a theatre of its suffering joy,
in fog coats and silk hats, cobbled the streets with seashells.

Wrested from its own hand a higher love,
so a blessed hour arrives and half of us is born,

a leaven of dry leaves climbs to its taste,
an unbidden silence where lilies give up their ghosts.

Before its own heart breaks, thrumming like a small quail,
a rattle of wind bends to its likeness,

and from its granite lips, a restless sin,
as light is its tavern and curfew its song.

As the black rose sings

My own infamy in the conversation
I have with the rose

Or Blake who tells us a bird can't soar too high
with its own wings.

In the orchid's mischief, chiselled cautionary tales
courting a frugal song

And a young boy imitating the carriage of blue
that swam like a sky.

Where I talk to the hours of crows
long into the tales of the cobalt night

Left evenly to my true work, flailing
on pinions of porcelain and string.

Singing a poem on skids of shining thoughts
a laughing Buddha, in the cellar-nest

Christ owning the tree and the flower shop
the hound of dead and living saddhus.

And the old one on the side of a hill
who cries like a loon in its blood and fog

And the whole of the unfaithful
on the edge of air, sailing there.

To know the hour at last,
the vanguard of hushed frightful distances,

The ghosted white of a hibiscus,
the black of the rose, its penitentiary song.

A kopeck for the gods

Beauty cries to its master
and I kiss your hand.

You are any stranger at all
and all my tears are for this alone.

The bramble of giant sunflowers made crown,
Goethe in his night clothes brooming the sun.

The touch-me-nots circling the seeker's way
spinners that bruise the cornsilk sky.

Costumes of wig trees in a sleepless chant,
burning their many coloured flags.

The matchmaker of yellow and blue
with her knotted ball of string,.

A kopeck for the gods,
echoing the birth of scriptural green.

Gilgamesh

When it rained burning chariots fell
The Fool of the world ran to the orchards.

The flame on the river and orchestras trembling, fled,
At night when the moon slept, I guarded the poor box.

Odin's two black ravens, the ash of Gilgamesh,
And the sound of the wheel turning with the sonnets of an oafish rain.

Pray to the constellations, the Gnostic queens,
The artists who throw colours on the canvas and hiss like the scathing of cats.

The old women once young, with white stallions,
Now sick, sick by my side, where will you go my songs

Who watched her arched back lift into a sail
The burning pyre of one breath

The wisdom beneath wisdom
And all of it quietly asking its way.

Chaikhana

for Alx

In the small honey chapel the winds stir the wine
If it is only a sacred circle made of stone, a morsel of breath, *who will know its taste*
And when bad news arrives, like a half moon, the good angel appears,
Tardy and fleeting, the clock's heart heavy, wringing its hands with time.

It may be only a word, watching the old ones feeding the birds,
A glimpse of wives' tales at the end of days, trolling the voiceless
So lovers hold a little tighter the space between them,
A tininess peers through their hands, a sail of silver lining.

You once told me about the green of a tree, how it was weeping everywhere
A poem in the flea market speaking more than the fig of silence
Songs on death row turning the maple red, the lacework of a moth's wing
The pleated skirt of a runaway star, the grey moment of saturnalia.

Now you are part of it, the stillness of barn owls has crept into your sweeping heart
You are looking everywhere at once for the same bruised sound, *who goes there it asks.*
In the small hours I remember a pale horse, riding a mounting field, in the doula of bright water
Look further, the small book is a great sun, standing tall before its shadow, *love asking love.*

The chime of bells climbing vines, late summer for a moment spreads its wings
It is red again, the agape love, the ghostly ward you are, running up the hill
You are not yet yoked, but to your own dreaming, many lives slowing, ending into one,
It is as I had seen, nothing is easy or hard, nothing better or worse than what is.

You have come far, homeward yes, but not an inch more than is allotted
Be the arrow that you are, humbly moving in the calm dance of what is still
On the long road from here to here, the teahouse is a place where every mystic gathers
Forgetting how they arrived, what they are not, and knowing they were never born.

The untitled way

for Dylan Thomas

The common starlight, rope laddered in that old nag's hair,
a rag shop of secrecy, dovetailed in time
falling in love with a loveliness,
in sing with the springtail of night.

What wanders there in a bird's hollow bones
brightly falling in the wiles and folly that follow the sailor's knot of missing song
a shoelace of red-fleeced golden word
horsetails in the candlewick shadows.

A jib of beating wings swept away in a salted smile
a tiny clutch of tiny wind in its talon,
slouched cats and blooming feather wands
rumours for a sleeping small horizon.

And things unseen tilting in our hands,
an hourglass of tillers cleaving the love-hounded painted circus
in the sunlight of their blood, the fancy trowels in a buoying greenish field,
a fog bell whistling in the black eye of night.

Dipping their nets, they hear only the sea speckled in pride
mending the barrios of a grand and open sky,
what betrays itself, at last, in the bruised and busking earth
that commonwealth which lovers lie upon, rumpled in time about.

Blind as mirrors that grim laughters chase
under the tail feather of bright moons slowly rising
darting tongues and black umbrellas rise, that writhe beneath rainbows
not yet born, as the stars look on its colourless aggregate.

And soldiers, come home to their command, favourite sons
while drunken lovers in charge of the stars look on,
and born there without labour, pass on her muck of light
in its crawlspace of good faith and shadow.

Bird swept, passing the torch, and the weather of good shelter
sing praises for the signatory of a wishing parliament
raindrops and limericks, severed from Christ's own hand
the spiralling note that catches in our throats and leaves us caught.

Then give me words for what we cannot praise,
and let secrets bleed our bleeding hearts away,
and there against the sound of clemency
plant fear into the grid of a songbird's mouth.

The dead names don't change, the scribe of such tiny things
and all the adorations lay low in the vineyard years
to keep his other's keeper, who kept fellowship with county flowers
and the common decency of the bard.

In the still house, the wee hours creeping, starlight about swirling head
bent above the sugars and soft footed heels
grief hobbling on its bone-weary cane, hear it tapping on the tin roof
where sin washes itself away, a penny traded for the sorrow of its song.

Rising beneath the shipwrecked sounds
in bits and pieces, and a child's shining buckled eyes
a tailspin of town criers and haggling sunrise, unsounded by love alone
when at last we have become that very silence.

Churchless coming

for Larkin

To know the pitter-patter of musty sounds, the old barn is best
the frightful distances where an hour must be climbed
to remove the sparrow from the bale branch
and the song from the singer's lips, catching an angel at last.

High oath holding lanterns in shepherds' fields, hand lettering the sheet glass
where steeples carve their way, skyless in spruce,
almost blue, and in weed grass and ingots of hymns
runaway summer brides, listening to the eyeless spaces.

In the tiny chapel that it is, nets a sash of dust, a wooded pew,
the church mouse, a small stowaway, in the castle of quiets that launders there
in sloughs of sins amid the skids of lust,
wicks the weeping rustle, the hollow witching of the heart.

The perfect limericks of frost painting cobwebs on window panes,
where a child sings the gift of copied treasure,
a spark of twigs unbundled
the fossil of the quicksilver caught in the flirting contest of leaves.

While deconstructed go all the tides, a wordsmith without a word,
even now in disbelief, a teacher's moon,
caught in the tattle of a river
that thoughtlessly perfects the wretched light.

And we write on as though imagination were true enough to be scripture,
wandering the smallish hours, dwarfing the paths,
a cold snap of weather without title,
half way above the below, where the dew of sun abides.

Here sleeping in the heart of every gypsy moth, a spinnery of green holy basal,
feather white asters, lovely as love lost,
a well bucket to pale away the spool of woolly eyes,
that finds in everywhere tininess to parade.

Every night when it rips my bones, and I do not hide,
the hidden arrives in its swath of honeyed gold,
and you and I silken-arrowed kissing what staggers above,
bathed in a cup of end more than beginning where a milk thought appears.

The horsemen on the steppe of each century
that must say its farewell to the bard of its fruitlessness,
and what can no longer be deceived,
into something other than itself.

A beautiful illusion, that chimney sweeps the shine of every feckless living thing,
the spelling bee of stillness that libels the lively dance
swift as a shadow and as suddenly unrobed,
a fading sweetness falling from the strawberry bramble work.

Before my very eyes, tractates of a whisky song, drag tones of the human tragedy,
comfortably alone, no heir for its divine anarchy,
no peerage for the near of far, the whistle of a feather falling, soundless
urgently visible, modestly taken in stride.

A council house of rag mills and rickshaw pullers pulling the starlight
from the sureness of the stars,
and a metronomic silence ringing in our ears,
not yet small enough to know its hour at last.

Song

My cup runneth over with emptiness
what can I remember of its generous command.

A caricature dreaming the pure elemental energy of the body
bounding across a canyon, my hand yet a constellation of stars.

Where did you die my song, though I did not,
writing poems from lovers' and hospital beds,

And sang in Havana, prophetically against the windmills that tilted in America's eye,
swaddled in trumpet flowers, a thiefdom of black-eyed kings.

I have studied with the great rabbis
and found the small bird huddled at Lorca's feet.

Where now is that voice in this dying body, slowly to be unseen
still a centurion, a light-hearted instrument, that litters the bruised sounds,

Croesus with his pale yellow treasure, pinions scraping the sky
small seeds growing into planets, and being human at last.

Sex, beauty, death, and yes, god, these I pursued, lovers uncountable deconstructed
into the burned-out cities that make a rose of every feared eye.

The spell of me grew wide, and birds listened, my ears opened like Assisi
and sometimes like a small Christ, I kissed beggars' hands, washed their feet with my tears.

And gave up my life for the stranger it was
prostrated before the tall-telling of an undying scribe.

Shallow hats tip in the shielding frost, the parade of evening rule,
the softness that raises every flag, swans in the afterlife.

A mule cart comes my way, one of death's angels,
the miniature circus of suffering tugs at my sleeve.

The oracle in the cutting gash, the glass shards shattered suddenly into praise,
the lost wing of moonlight, lingering in a prolix of evening tide,

The clouds draping a bare-headed sun, burning in the books
the Andalusian blue that cannot be untold

That ashed-out song in the poorest of envies,
and the poems, an indescribable word for god.

Shoreless

Here is my bid, to feast on a word that is famished
The glowing dew that listens like a fallen drop of rain
On an unsighted leaf, the chaste universe, smitten by earth
And in the high pastures, where tribes of angels gather.

And over there, a splintering treasure, ambulant from above
The ether in thin air, that quietly moves the creaseless note
Weaving a wand of music, so deftly, only the puffed up moonlight can hear
How is it, that warriors and seekers die on both sides of the tireless shore.

Knowing not what line will last, not a single word, but only this
We call by name, returned, half alive, half begging, leaping from sky to sky
For a coin that might uncrown, at last, a ripened thought
A word that blooms like a slowly nodding flower, buffing the eternal night.

Lovers lie in the grass, playing a child's games, death haunts old men
Who carry this dream like a fool, and mutter to themselves their last hours
While everywhere suffering tightens the reigns, star loops in far and broken places
Until we see, tethered in the death ground of the heart, the poem's true face.

Glance by glance, every spring of unconstructed sight unseen
In the tree boughs, hellhound on the coattails of the invisible,
Every thatched and buttoned roof of love, old cloth maps deifying the rivers,
Reeling in its knotted rope of weather, the tender books of covenant.

Eternal I say, though it passes, like the shadow of a fly, its wings in my hand
And we draw whatever story we can, by the step of mind
As motionless we are struck, a stroke of a painter's brush turned song
Motioned away by the colours, and the words, too many times mentioned, that are one.

GRATITUDE

Rafi, for the ten years you missed my driveway, but managed to fulfill the first pillar of the Navajo creed (show up), and in loving devotion, the other three that follow.

My nephew, more of a son, Alex, who's heart and blood are my own, for simply being in the world, lending his beautiful loving and nascent writer's eye.

To my student, Lefteri Alexander (Alx), a son in spiritus, for his rigour and the immensity of love, singing the wish list that is forever begging a song.

Meyer, my oldest friend, who honoured, in the vigil of overcoming his own suffering, the work and words, that is the abode of love.

My brother, who listened deeply to nascent versions of a number of these poems.

Dwane, for unerringly turning the music off at the coffee shop, gracefully at the mystic hour, for so many years.

Ben and Esther, who each believe and lovingly support in their own way the work.

Al Moritz, for his deep generosity and eloquence, in writing a few words to ineffably describe that one word in which every other appears.

And to Michael and all those at Exile, who first solicited the manuscript, honouring and graciously gifting its passage.

Lastly, my small Buddha cat who watched over me, and the poems, as one who watches the one watching the watcher.

ACKNOWLEDGEMENTS

Many of these poems have been published and were either recipients of, or short listed for, a variety of awards. The title poem and full suite "In a Time of No Song" received the 2014 Gwendolyn MacEwan Award for Poetry. "Dovesellers" was selected for an award in the Cardiff International Competition (Academi, Wales), and published in the New Welsh Review. "Hunchback" was selected as part of an anthology in 2011, by Glyn Maxwell, and performed live at the Greenwich Theatre in London, England; and "Tahrir Square" was selected as a 2011 *Arc* Poem of the Year Editor's Choice Award. "Squaw duck for the bard" was short listed for the 2010 Arvon Award by Britain's poet laureate, Carol Ann Duffy. The poetry suites "History of the Unknown World" and "Last Angels" were short listed for the CBC Literary Awards, and "From the Book of Angels" and "Tilandsias" for the Winston Collin's/*Descant* award. A selection of poems were awarded an Ontario Arts Council grant to be recorded to musical compositions, and others have been broadcast in Canada and internationally. In 2013, Mercan Dede composed music to "Hafiz" and other pieces, taking their place on the album alongside poems by Rumi and a rare recording of Gandhi. "Poems" and several other selections will be published in a special hand pressed edition, by Mark C. Murray at the bindery and studio, New York.